SPECIAL LIBRARIES

A Guide for Management

Fourth Edition

Cathy A. Porter
Mary E. Beall
Janice F. Chindlund
Rebecca S. Corliss
Christina M. Krawczyk
Sara R. Tompson
Lorri A. Zipperer

Janice F. Chindlund

Special Libraries Association

Washington, DC
1997

The Economist Intelligence Unit
The Economist Building
111 West 57th Street
New York, NY 10019, USA
Telephone: 212-554-0600

SLA gratefully acknowledges The Economist Intelligence Unit, sponsor of the Nonserial Publications program.

1700 Eighteenth Street, NW
Washington, DC 20009-2514, USA
1-202-234-4700
www.sla.org

Manufactured in the United States of America.

Library of Congress Cataloging-in-Publication Data
Special libraries : a guide for management / Cathy A. Porter ... [et al.]. — 4th ed.
p. cm.
Rev. ed. of: Special libraries / Elin B. Christianson. 3rd ed. 1991
Includes bibliographical references and index.
ISBN 0-87111-466-6
1. Special libraries—United States—Administration.
I. Porter, Cathy A. II. Christianson, Elin B. Special libraries.
Z675.A2C53 1997 97-8193
026—dc21 CIP

Contents

Preface

This book traditionally has been a guide not only for managers, but for librarians and students new to the field of special libraries. To our great delight, the literature on special librarianship has expanded in the 1990s to the point where special librarians and library school students have a myriad of books and articles to read and study to help them become better librarians. Many of these are published by the Special Libraries Association. For this reason, we, the new team of writers and editors of this book, have shifted our focus back to the original intent—to inform management, that is, non-librarians, about who special librarians are, what they do, and how their work benefits any organization with a need to manage information. In this day of wildly expanding and changing information resources, just about every kind of organization imaginable needs to manage information.

We hope you will find the fourth edition informative, easy-to-read, and relatively free of cryptic library jargon. In the appendices, we have included a glossary of those terms and concepts important to understanding information management and what a special library does. We have also included a list of further reading for those of you who want to delve deeper into special librarianship, as well as chapter bibliographies of sources that deal with each chapter's topic in greater detail. We have also included some readings that examine current thinking on how businesses should utilize and value information.

In several sections of the *Guide* we have also cited URLs for pages on the World Wide Web. The exact addresses may change, as the Web is notoriously fluid at the present time. We wanted our readers, however, to be aware of the resources found there, and trust that search engines will make it possible to locate these pages in spite of any future address changes.

A WORD ABOUT TERMINOLOGY

Organizations with special libraries call them by many different names. They have been called the information center, research center, information research center, business library, research library, corporate library, and information services department, among other things. They take any name that works well within the organizations they serve, but in this book we refer to them all as *special libraries*.

Special librarians were among the first in the business world to consider the colleagues in their organizations who used their services as customers. We have chosen to name these internal customers *users* to avoid confusion with the external customers or clients who purchase or receive the services of the organization as a whole.

ACKNOWLEDGMENTS

Special librarians network and share constantly, making it impossible to thank every individual who contributed to the discussions surrounding this book, so we would like to send a comprehensive thank you to our colleagues in the Illinois Chapter of the Special Libraries Association. We would also like to thank the American Library Association's library staff. Particular individuals who assisted us in various ways were Brenda Barerra; Wayne Hoppe, Esquire; David Hirschey, Esquire; and Sandy Won.

We thank our families and friends for their support, and our mentors and colleagues at work who helped shape the ideas you see reflected in these pages, including Stephen P. Bonine, Brian Boyd, K. V. Chindlund, Sheila Collins, Karin Donahue, Rebecca Edmunds, Mat Krawczyk, Kathy Kren, John C. Rivard, Holly Stedman, Ross Vagnieres, and Kevin W. Williams.

Saving the best for last, our deepest gratitude to the previous editors, Elin B. Christianson, David E. King, and Janet L. Ahrensfeld for bringing us together and giving us this opportunity to share our enthusiasm for the work we do.

Why Read This Book?

Most people don't know that special libraries exist, much less what they do. Even in organizations that have them, there is often a lack of real understanding of the library's function and what it contributes to the organization. Why should anyone care? The answer is that special libraries and the information professionals who manage them provide an increasingly important service to the organizations they serve.

Estimates indicate that knowledge doubles every ten to twelve years.[1] Articles in the business press lament a lack of know-how in managing the current "information explosion." One recent editorial declared: "Someone needs to manage information in organizations. We have plenty of people whose job is to manage information technology . . . But whose job is it to help people determine their information needs when a computer system isn't the preferred information medium? Who monitors available information resources in the company? In most cases, the answer is nobody."[2]

The author goes on to list the desired characteristics for the job: "a broad business understanding and knowledge of the organization's structure and function; knowledge of the organization's diverse sources and uses of information; facility with information technology; being politically astute but capable of leadership; strong interpersonal skills; and orientation to business performance improvement rather than internal functional goals."[3]

What the author of this article has described is a good special librarian. Special librarians know that the need is not to create a new information function, but to adapt the existing one to the changing information environment. Special libraries developed in the early part of this century when resources were predominantly in print format. Because of this, their role was to collect, classify, and store print materials. This is still how many people view libraries. But a library's functions and services have grown and changed along with the development of information retrieval technologies, to the point where some libraries now operate with little or no physical collections at all.

Special Libraries: A Guide for Management explains what special libraries and librarians do, what skills librarians have to offer, and how the services they provide can be applied in a business environment, both inside and outside of a library facility, to benefit almost any organization. Each year scores of organizations ask the Special Libraries Association for information and guidance in establishing special libraries. This book was originally written to provide a broad outline of answers to the most frequently asked questions. It is directed primarily to the individual or group of individuals who have been charged with the task of finding solutions to the organization's information problems. The *Guide* can also be of use to organizations that wish to evaluate information services already in operation. The basic questions we addressed are

What is a special library?

When is an organization ready for a special library?

How does the special library work within the organization?

What does the special library do?

Where does the information come from?

How is the information organized?

How does the information get to the user?

Who staffs the special library?

What space and equipment are needed?

How much will the special library cost?

What other roles can information professionals play in an organization?

If you are new to the concept of special libraries, we recommend that you read the first four chapters to get a basic understanding of what librarians in the special library setting do and how their work can benefit an organization. We hope these chapters will convince you to contact a special librarian and let them handle the rest. If you want more detail about the planning, everyday operations, and cost considerations of a special library, the remaining chapters provide a basic overview.

LITERATURE CITED

1. Walter B. Wriston, "The State of American Management," *Harvard Business Review* 68, no. 1 (January-February 1990): 80.
2. Tom Davenport, "Functions Worth Following," *InformationWeek* no. 527 (15 May 1995): 158.
3. Ibid.

CHAPTER

1

What Is a Special Library?

> *"As the Information Age unfolds, more and more of what people buy, sell, and do has knowledge as its raw material..."*[1]

It's Friday afternoon and the vice president of communications needs information within the hour in order to respond to the media regarding a crisis situation occurring in the Pacific Rim.

A competitor is gaining market share. Information on its products and strategy is needed to combat the situation.

A fast-paced department is having difficulty organizing (storing, indexing and retrieving) the documents it produces. These documents are needed to move ahead on important projects.

A new strategic initiative is underway. Analysis of past and current research is necessary to begin the initiative.

How do people in business and professional organizations acquire the information necessary for their work? Thousands of organizations in need of information turn to information professionals and their libraries for the information they need. Nowhere is information more important than in the world of business and the professions, where quality of information used in planning, producing, and distributing goods and services, is central to success. Special libraries, so called because their focus is more defined or specialized than public or academic libraries, are an important source of information, and they play significant roles in channeling work-related information in their parent organizations. Although special libraries may be known by a variety of names (e.g. corporate library, research center, information center), they all share common characteristics and goals.

GOALS AND CHARACTERISTICS

WHAT IS THEIR MISSION?

The mission of special libraries is to provide focused information to a defined group of users on an ongoing basis to further the mission and goals of their parent organizations. It is the reason that "Putting Knowledge to Work" was chosen as the slogan of the Special Libraries Association.

WHERE ARE THEY LOCATED?

Special libraries exist in a wide variety of organizational settings, including financial institutions, science and technology firms, research and development centers, consulting firms, marketing and advertising agencies, cultural and government agencies, hospitals, law firms, and associations. Special libraries may or may not have books or even a physical location. A special library is increasingly being defined more by its mission than by its floor space and collections.

WHO USES THEM?

Special libraries serve a well-defined group of users. The users range from the staff of a single department to employees throughout the organization. Some special libraries, such as those maintained by trade or professional associations, consider the association's membership, or anyone with a serious interest in the subject, as part of their user base.

WHAT IS THEIR FOCUS?

Special libraries are oriented to a single subject or several related subjects. This subject scope is determined by the field of activity and interests of the library's parent organization. Thus, special libraries are often described in terms of their subject orientation: advertising and marketing, business, finance, law, pharmaceutical, electronics, aerospace, chemistry, medical, or dental libraries. Some are best described in terms of a form of material or information; picture libraries and patent libraries are examples. Still others are most aptly described in terms of their parent organizations: museum, hospital, or newspaper libraries. The common characteristic is an orientation to materials and information that is specialized rather than general in character.

WHO MANAGES THEM?

It is the professional librarian's expertise in managing information and working with users to identify, anticipate, and satisfy their information needs that transforms a passive collection into an information system used to support business decisions. A special library cannot exist without a librarian, and is only as good as the information professional managing it and the level of support and commitment from the parent organization. This professional has two primary roles: information expert and resource manager.

THE ROLE OF THE SPECIAL LIBRARIAN

THE INFORMATION EXPERT

Information retrieval. The special librarian has a thorough knowledge of information resources; how, why, and for whom they are produced, and where to find them. Providing users with specialized information *from* a variety of sources (print, CD-ROM, online, interviews, networking) *through* a variety of vehicles (print, conversation, team participation, e-mail, fax, internal electronic databases, or knowledgebases) is the essential function of the special librarian. The special librarian not only knows where information resides and how to find it, but also how to evaluate its quality and timeliness. This includes obscure and sometimes unpublished information, which is particularly important in the area of competitive intelligence. Put simply, a librarian is trained in the research techniques necessary to locate the best information in the least time at the lowest cost.

Knowledge management. As an expert in information organization, retrieval, and dissemination, the special librarian can also be commissioned with the role of knowledge manager. In this role the librarian develops a process to discover the sources of intellectual capital within an organization and to index, store, and design easy retrieval systems. These two roles, managing retrieval of *external* information or knowledge, and managing organization and retrieval of *internal* information or knowledge, are merging to an increasing degree.

Information consultant. Working with users and groups such as cross-functional teams, librarians leverage their information expertise and are often an integral part of project planning and implementation. By listening to the needs of the organization and articulating the capabilities of information resources to meet them, the information professional keeps users and management up-to-date regarding resources and services available to meet the needs of the organization, both inside and outside of the library.

Information purchasing agent. Working from the consulting role described above, the librarian can combine knowledge of the organization's needs, expertise in information resources, and familiarity with information vendors, to act as an agent or liaison for purchasing materials and automated information delivery systems for the organization as a whole. Library purchasing procedures can be configured to handle purchases for everyone and take advantage of volume discounts offered by many vendors.

Training. To an increasing degree, the role of the special librarian is that of educator, teaching members of the organization how to be the best possible information consumers. As noted by Stan Davis and Jim Botkin, "Over the next few decades, the private sector will eclipse the public sector as our predominant educational institution."[2] Special librarians teach end users how to tap information sources, such as online databases, CD-ROMs, and the Internet, as well as a variety of other sources, and how to evaluate the information they find. Special librarians strive and thrive when they are continually learning and possess an insatiable curiosity, and understand the importance of sharing their knowledge.

Information technology. An appreciation for technology, even an affinity for learning all one can about it, is a prerequisite for special librarianship today. As heavy end users of information retrieval technology since the age of dumb terminals, acoustic modems, and arcane command language search engines, special librarians can be the perfect liaison between system designers and end users. They also have extensive exposure to the way in which end users approach information queries. As a result, special librarians are able to provide valuable insight in the design of databases, knowledgebases of internal intellectual capital, and home pages on intranets and the Internet.

THE RESOURCE MANAGER

Managing people, budgets, technology, and expectations, the information professional leverages resources to accomplish the organization's goals. From the choice of which sources to use to fulfill a particular research request to the acquisition of resources to the hiring of staff, the special librarian is a decision maker.

Information planning. Vision is necessary to position the information function as the organization and technology change. Involving librarians at the onset of planning strategic or marketing initiatives ensures that the information needed to make fact-based decisions is readily available and that the knowledge gained during the process can be stored for future reference. With awareness of the past, a sense of urgency in the present, and a vision for the future, the special librarian molds the plans for the information function with management, based on the needs of the users and the mission of the organization.

Networking. Networking is the quintessential skill of the special librarian. The special librarian partners with users, vendors, and other special libraries to obtain the information necessary to fulfill the organization's information needs. As an interpreter of the organization's mission, the information professional communicates that mission to users and vendors. Listening to user requests, refining the requests, and reporting results in easy-to-understand terms are communication skills routinely employed by special librarians. Communicating the parameters of information needs of the organization to vendors is imperative to defining the role vendors play in developing the tools that provide needed answers.

Change management. Adaptability and flexibility are key to the librarian's role. The librarian is at the forefront of change management whenever a new or improved system affecting information storage and retrieval is developed. For instance, instituting a knowledge management system where users are asked to share their work or the conclusions drawn from a project in an electronic setting requires changes in behavior. The librarian anticipates and plans for the changes these new expectations will require.

Management asks and answers many tough questions in order to determine the direction for their organization. Asking the right questions of the right people leads to an information advantage. A professional at the helm of a special library can help provide that advantage. Experienced special librarians have the training, expertise, skills, connections, and vision to help an organization effectively use information.

LITERATURE CITED

1. Thomas A. Stewart, "Mapping Corporate Brainpower," *Fortune* 132, no. 9 (30 October 1995): 209.
2. Stan Davis and Jim Botkin, "The Coming of Knowledge-Based Business," *Harvard Business Review* 72, no. 5 (September-October 1994): 170.

CHAPTER

2

When Is an Organization Ready for a Special Library?

> *"The information deluge can drown you, but if you organize it well, it can be a powerful tool."*[1]

Information is key in today's business environment. More information is available through an increasing variety of technologies, more information is required to effectively compete, and the process of supplying the right information to the right people without overwhelming them or missing critical facts is increasingly complex. Many organizations have long understood these issues; others are reaching a critical point and beginning to recognize the need to address them. The most important factors in the decision to manage information effectively are management support and their commitment of the resources required to effectively manage information.

The events that move an organization to this decision are as varied as the organizations themselves. There are certain common situations or problems that lead management to realize that an organized effort in a central facility, i.e. a special library, would improve its operations and benefit the overall knowledge culture of the organization. This chapter identifies some of those common conditions.

THE RECOGNITION OF NEEDS

When management recognizes one or more of the following problems, and seeks solutions to them, the organization is ready for a special library.

1. There is a lack of awareness of, and control over, the information resources held by the organization.

   - Redundant research is conducted or purchased by multiple departments.
   - Duplicate copies of books and periodicals, and multiple contracts with database vendors, are purchased without method or consideration of the cost benefits of group contracts.
   - Information resources are scattered throughout the organization, available only to those who happen to know of their existence and whereabouts. Needed materials cannot be located, as there is no control over their storage, distribution, or use.

     According to studies sponsored by the National Science Foundation and the Department of Energy, an estimated $10 billion was saved because scientists and engineers were able to obtain articles and technical reports they needed from libraries. Researchers estimated it would cost about 40% more of their time to locate needed materials if a library were not available, thus resulting in a 10% loss of productivity.[2]

   - Intellectual capital, that is, internal research and employee experience, is scattered or exists in the memory of long-term employees, who are often overworked due to the reliance on their knowledge. When they are busy, that knowledge is inaccessible; when these employees leave it goes with them.

     A recent survey of sixty for-profit and not-for-profit organization executives found that nearly half felt their awareness of their internal knowledge base was not effective.

> Nearly three quarters admitted a lack of awareness of promising knowledge centers by upper management.[3]

2. The amount of potential information is great but there is a lack of knowledge about information sources and information technology.
   - No coordinated effort is made to inform staff of new publications, news services, databases, or free resources that would provide relevant information for their work.
   - Access to electronic databases is purchased and end users are trained to use them, but little guidance is offered regarding the scope of their content and how they can be used.
   - The variety of forms in which information is offered—print, microform, online, CD-ROM, and Internet—is overwhelming. No one has the time to investigate which forms are best for the organization's needs.
   - Some of the larger, more sophisticated resources are too expensive for individual departments to purchase on their own. No central authority is in place to identify common needs across departments or to manage the vendor contracts.

3. Information gathering is inefficient and incomplete.
   - Managers and employees are increasingly aware that they cannot keep up with published literature in their field of expertise. To add to the frustration, much of what they do receive is late, duplicated in multiple sources, erroneous, or in a format that they can't use.
   - Actionable information is delayed, resulting in loss of opportunity. As a result, competitors beat the organization in the marketplace.
   - Decisions are delayed because of a lack of correct information. Someone discovers information that would have altered an earlier decision, or makes a bad decision based on inept research.

   > In a widely-circulated medical journal, two medical professionals questioned the need for another specialized medical journal, based on a MEDLINE search showing

> less than 120 articles within the scope of the new journal. A medical librarian, well versed in the correct methods of searching MEDLINE, used the original authors' methodology to refute the claim, finding almost 14,000 articles on the subject. The original statement was poorly researched and erroneous, undermining the authors' reputations as researchers.[4]

- Employees spend an inordinate amount of time trying to locate usable information, thus diminishing the time they have to apply it—if they find it—to their work.
- Employees find electronic databases difficult to use or search them infrequently, forgetting more complex search techniques. As a result they incur large online fees, fail to extract needed information from them, and turn to easier, less appropriate sources.
- Labor intensive primary research is undertaken that has been conducted elsewhere and reported in a publicly available source.

> A consultant needed production figures for bottle caps. A research assistant spent days searching for the information unaware that it was available in a $2 government report.[5]

THE COMMITMENT OF RESOURCES

Once an organization decides it cannot afford inefficient information management, it must devote careful thought to what resources it can commit to improving this situation through the development and continued funding of a special library. Space considerations, funding allocations, personnel requirements, and information needs must be explored and documented so the decision makers can see the validity of the enterprise.

An information initiative culminating in a library requires team planning. An information professional should be consulted from the beginning, either as an employee or a consultant, to see that all the concerns involved are addressed. Administrators and managers involved with the information flow of the organization should be members of this team. Their participation in developing the library's objectives and services ensures that the library meets the organization's needs. Participants also learn what the library can do, enabling them to provide management support throughout the life of the library. Some organizations continue to have a formal library committee to keep the information staff informed as to changing user needs and developments within the organization, and the management informed of developments in information management.

It is imperative that, from its inception, the library be adequately funded and staffed, with room in the proposed budget to allow it to grow and change with the organization. Careful examination of the functions and needs of the library, as outlined in the subsequent chapters of this book, provides a basis for determining the level of support necessary to meet information service goals, and assist in wise investment of the time and financial resources of the organization.

CHALLENGES

A manager starting an information management initiative should be ready to address potential obstacles, many of which are very familiar to special librarians.

- It is difficult to quantify library service and its value to an organization.
- Special libraries can be costly, long term undertakings.
- It is difficult to generate significant income from a library, even those with fee-based services.
- Information services have to be carefully and adequately marketed to users to obtain their patronage and support.
- Upper level management is often unaware of information issues and problems as they are not usually involved in doing research—their subordinates do it for them.
- Management does not always understand the skills involved in effective information retrieval, sometimes assuming that providing their staff with a few end user databases is enough.

A trained information professional, consulted from the beginning, aids in identifying potential pitfalls and preparing to deal with them.

An organization's information weaknesses should be documented as they become apparent. Special librarians should survey knowledge workers in the organization for concrete examples of problems or deficiencies that support the creation of a library. Keep track of the costs of any outside information services used. Tangible examples of the issues and problems discussed in this chapter should be identified. With careful preparation, the value of organized information management should become apparent. In a study of banking libraries, "over 99 percent of the 229 executives surveyed responded that the information provided by the company libraries is current, accurate, valuable and has contributed to better decisions."[6]

The Special Libraries Association provides consultants and materials that help identify the need for a library and document the case in a manner that is both understandable and meaningful to the decision makers of the organization. Contact information for this and other library organizations with a more specific subject focus can be found in the appendices to this book.

LITERATURE CITED

1. William H. Miller, "Leadership at a Crossroads," *Industry Week* 245, no. 15 (19 August 1996), 44.
2. "Library Copies Save Big Bucks," *American Libraries* 17, no 2 (February 1986): 96.
3. Tom Lester, "Intellectual Capital: Core Asset for the Third Millennium," *Financial Times*, 9 August 1996.
4. Ira and Linda Katz, "Geriatric Psychiatry and the Limits of MeSH," Letter to the Editor, *Journal of the American Medical Association* 274, no. 19 (15 November 1995): 1508.
5. Johnnie L. Roberts, "As Information Swells, Firms Open Libraries," *Wall Street Journal*, 26 September 1983, 1.
6. Mary Lee Kennedy, "Positioning Strategic Information: Partnering for the Information Advantage," *Special Libraries* 87, no 2 (Spring 1996): 122.

FURTHER READING

Marshall, Joanne G. *The Impact of the Special Library on Corporate Decision-Making*. Washington, DC: Special Libraries Association, 1993.

Owens, Ian, Tom Wilson, and Angela Abell. *Information and Business Performance: A Study of Information Systems and Services in High Performing Companies*. London: Bowker-Saur, 1996.

CHAPTER

3

How Does the Special Library Work Within the Organization?

"Strategically developing and deploying an information environment that is relevant, reliable and timely requires senior management commitment, vision, leadership and cross-disciplinary teamwork."[1]

Planning the special library is a collaborative process within the organization. It is carried out through consultation and decision making by the managing librarian, the potential users of the library, and the managers concerned with information needs and services. This interaction is a critical element in identifying information needs, setting library goals, and identifying the resources necessary for the successful establishment of the library. It is important to recognize that while the most intensive period of planning and consideration of the library's objectives will take place when the library is established and during the first year or so of its existence, the responsibilities and objectives of the library should be reviewed periodically and revised in accordance with advances in technology and changes in the organization's activities. Continual evaluation of the organization's objectives and goals is essential to keeping the library efficient, effective, and responsive to the organization's information needs.

THE INFORMATION AUDIT: WHAT ARE THE NEEDS OF THE ORGANIZATION?

The first step in planning the special library is to define clearly the goals and mission of the parent organization and to understand its information needs. To do this, the information professional conducts an information audit, or a series of interviews, to determine these goals and needs. Some questions the librarian might ask include the following.

- What is the primary product or service of this organization?
- What kinds of information services are needed to support production or improve productivity?
- Who would be the primary users of the library?
- Where should the special library be positioned within the organization to be most effective?

STRUCTURING THE LIBRARY TO ACHIEVE GOALS

After conducting the initial information audit, the special librarian designs library services with the following considerations in mind.

ORGANIZATIONAL PLACEMENT

The librarian and management need to determine which employees or departments will use and benefit most from information services. Carefully defining the user group will help determine the most appropriate organizational placement and reporting structure for the library. The library in a department or division usually reports to the head of that unit. If the library is a separate unit providing service to a broad range of departments, it may report to an appropriate administrator, such as the chief executive of the organization, the Chief Information Officer, or the head of administrative services. One executive recommends, "try to find a group with executives who have a clear need for varied information combined with an orientation that allows them to appreciate and value information as a worthy resource."[2]

LOCATION

Location depends on whether the library serves the entire organization, a specific unit, or several related units. If it serves the whole organization, it may be located in the central office, close to the administrative functions of the organization. If it serves a particular unit or office, it should be located at the same site for easy access by its primary users. If the library will be serving multiple locations, communications must be facilitated by dedicated phone, fax, and network (electronic mail) connections.

COMMUNICATION

Communications must flow between the library and its users regarding new organizational goals and challenges, and new library activities and solutions. To be most cost-effective and proactive, the library manager should be involved in planning and development activities in order to anticipate and prepare for information needs. Some organizations assign special librarians to be members of specific project teams.

SERVICES

The information audit will reveal what types of services an organization needs. The following are some of the questions that must be addressed.

- Will the library provide statistics and articles on an as-needed basis?
- Is the library expected merely to respond to users' requests, or proactively generate periodic reports on pertinent topics?
- Will the library gather and compile competitive intelligence on other companies or industries?
- How will the information be presented to users, i.e., will the library provide raw data, or analyze and synthesize it?
- Does the organization need a central repository or archive for company and project documents?
- Should the library centralize and coordinate the purchasing and dissemination of research materials?

HOURS AND TURNAROUND

What kind of turnaround time is expected? What projects take priority? How much staff is needed to complete projects in a timely manner, and what are the contingency plans for emergencies, rush projects, and overtime? These factors must be considered by the managing librarian when planning hours, staff, and services.

COST RECOVERY

In organizations where employees bill their time to clients, such as law and consulting firms, will the library's time and costs be billed as well, or will they be absorbed into administrative costs? Will only research projects and expenses be billed, or will all administrative functions such as ordering, paying bills, and marketing be assigned a billing amount as well? What will the billing rates be? Is the library responsible for submitting time sheets documenting all time spent on client work, as well as billing expenses to individual client or department accounts? Or will the library budget be allocated on an annual basis to the departments that use it? These considerations affect the work of the librarian and the perception of the library by the organization.

MARKETING

The special library may employ a variety of techniques to market existing and new services. These include giving orientation presentations to new employees, publishing a newsletter alerting users to new resources, and sponsoring tours and demonstrations of new technologies. Regular involvement with project teams enables the library staff to alert team members of new resources and technologies.

SURVEYS OF PERFORMANCE, VALUE, AND CHANGING NEEDS

In order to continue to provide the services an organization needs, the special library may survey its users on a regular basis. Surveys measure whether services are useful or needed, if the users have experienced better decision making or productivity as a result of using library assistance, and whether the library's practices still reflect the missions and goals of the organization. Special librarians must keep informed about the changing information needs of their organization, and must be able to adapt to new agendas.

In addition to the issues listed above, the special library manager and the organization need to consider the more specific questions of budget and staffing, which are discussed in later chapters. The most crucial consideration when planning the library's role in the organization is to make sure that the library's practices reflect the agendas and business environment of the parent organization. Different organizations need different levels of information service, which will be discussed in the next chapter. A careful information audit and periodic reviews result in a library that is tailored to effectively further the goals of its organization.

LITERATURE CITED

1. Mary Lee Kennedy, "Positioning Strategic Information: Partnering for the Information Advantage," *Special Libraries* 87, no. 2 (Spring 1996): 124.
2. Laurence Prusak, "Corporate Libraries: A Soft Analysis, A Warning, and Some Generic Advice" in *Information for Management: A Handbook*, ed. James Matarazzo and Miriam Drake (Washington, DC: Special Libraries Association, 1994), 81.

FURTHER READING

Brimsek, Tobi A., ed. *From the Top: Profiles of U. S. and Canadian Corporate Libraries and Information Centers.* Washington, DC: Special Libraries Association, 1989.

Inside Information: Profiles of Association Libraries and Information Centers. Washington, DC: Special Libraries Association, 1991.

Matarazzo, James. *Corporate Library Excellence.* Washington, DC: Special Libraries Association, 1990.

Special Libraries Association. *The Information Audit: An SLA Information Kit.* Washington, DC: Special Libraries Association, 1995.

CHAPTER

4

What Does the Special Library Do?

The kinds of services and activities undertaken by special libraries vary considerably. Few organizations can offer unlimited resources to the library operation, so it is important for the special librarian or information professional to establish objectives and priorities from the start. It is critically important to plan for resources adequate to achieve the organization's goals. Although exercising flexibility and seeking alternate ways of doing things are common practices among special librarians, the level of services provided will depend upon the resources for staff, budget, space, and equipment that are available for the library.

The concept of levels of service can be illustrated by selecting the three most important areas of library activity and describing how each of them might be performed at different levels of service. There are three functions that are central to the operation of all libraries, and which make the special library a unique service unit within an organization:[1]

- Acquisition—gathering information
- Organization—organizing and displaying the information
- Dissemination—making the information available to users

The following checklists describe these three functions in terms of three levels of service: **basic**, **intermediate**, and **maximum**. The level of service is dictated by the level of resources available. Having professional library staff to perform these functions is what differentiates a special library from a passive collection of information materials.

The checklists can serve as a benchmarking tool, which could prove useful for organizations setting up a new library and searching for performance goals or standards. Library services also can and should be measured using criteria that are applied to other service and resource units in the organization. Likewise, special librarians should be reviewed against the same criteria applied to other professionals within the organization.

ACQUIRING MATERIALS FOR THE LIBRARY

BASIC

As part of basic acquisition services, a special librarian usually performs the following functions.

- ❑ Keeps abreast of the organization's general interests and needs for information and materials.
- ❑ Collects publications scattered throughout the organization, receives in the library those publications that come automatically to the organization, and checks these materials to assure relevancy and to avoid duplication.
- ❑ Reviews announcements of new publications, selects basic materials, and orders them directly from the publisher.
- ❑ Establishes a simple order record.
- ❑ Provides access to computerized database, online, and Internet services appropriate to the interests of the organization.

INTERMEDIATE

At an intermediate, more active level of function, the special librarian adds or substitutes many of the following acquisitions services.

- ❑ Keeps informed about the developing information needs of the organization and selects resources in anticipation of the actual requirement for them.
- ❑ Reviews the library's collections and builds up weak areas.
- ❑ Prepares a written acquisition policy.
- ❑ Begins to acquire special collections of materials such as patents, internal reports, maps, and audiovisual materials such as photographs or video tapes as necessary.
- ❑ Handles journal subscriptions or book purchases for the entire organization.

- ❑ Creates and maintains a complete order file with automatic follow-up procedures.
- ❑ Establishes a regular system for checking with authorities within the organization for evaluations of material.
- ❑ Selects and provides access to specialized databases, Internet services, newswire services, etc.

MAXIMUM

At a maximum, proactive level of function, the special librarian adds or substitutes many of the following acquisitions services.

- ❑ Periodically does formal research concerning users' needs.
- ❑ Establishes contacts with experts and dealers of unusual publications, e.g. out-of-print, unpublished, or foreign.
- ❑ Adds other specialized collections, such as catalogs of executive development programs, training videos and materials, and archival materials of the organization.
- ❑ Purchases materials to meet information needs for special projects.

ORGANIZING MATERIALS IN THE LIBRARY

BASIC

As part of basic organization activities, the special librarian generally performs the following functions.

- ❑ Places books on shelves in a simple, logical order, for example, by author or by broad subject grouping.
- ❑ Arranges magazines and other periodicals by title and date.
- ❑ Establishes a filing system in which pamphlets, clippings, advertising pieces, and other ephemeral materials (short-lived in usefulness or composition) are organized by subject.
- ❑ Makes a card or computer record that identifies all major publications in the library by author or title.

INTERMEDIATE

As part of an intermediate level of organizing the collection, the special librarian adds or substitutes many of the following.

- ❑ Develops a card- or computer-based catalog with subject analysis.

- ❑ Adopts a published classification scheme and uses it for subject arrangement of books.
- ❑ Adopts a published subject heading list for cataloging books and for indexing the collection of pamphlets, clippings, and other materials in files.
- ❑ Devises specific filing and finding systems for special collections such as patents, maps, photographs, and slides.

MAXIMUM

At a maximum level of organizing the collection, the special librarian adds or substitutes many of the following.

- ❑ Creates internal subject organization systems tailored to the organization's needs, such as special classification schemes, expanded subject headings, or thesauri.
- ❑ Integrates internal and external databases.
- ❑ Indexes articles, reports, and other materials in depth using database management, text retrieval, and indexing software.
- ❑ Prepares abstracts of published materials.

DISSEMINATING INFORMATION AND MATERIALS FROM THE LIBRARY

BASIC

As part of a basic level of service in providing people with the information they need, a special librarian typically does the following.

- ❑ Maintains a collection of reference books and basic databases.
- ❑ Answers simple, factual questions.
- ❑ Identifies titles of publications and verifies references.
- ❑ Prepares a brochure or shared computer files, such as a World Wide Web page, describing the library's resources and services.
- ❑ Directs users needing detailed or research information to possible sources outside the library.
- ❑ Routes new issues of magazines, or the tables of contents thereof, to people who have requested them.
- ❑ Routes new incoming materials to staff members whose interests are known.
- ❑ Knows the resources of local libraries well enough for full utilization.

INTERMEDIATE

The special librarian more active in disseminating information adds or substitutes many of the following services.

- ❑ Gathers research materials pertinent to a question and transmits them to requesters.
- ❑ Expands public relations and marketing activities.
- ❑ Prepares selective bibliographies.
- ❑ Undertakes comprehensive literature searches on request.
- ❑ Distributes lists of current literature received, sometimes including abstracts from published sources.
- ❑ Has broad familiarity with national and global library resources in pertinent subject fields.
- ❑ Participates in cooperative library networks.

MAXIMUM

The special librarian providing maximum information dissemination services adds or substitutes many of the following.

- ❑ Locates, synthesizes, and evaluates information and provides it in written summary form.
- ❑ Prepares critical bibliographies.
- ❑ Prepares evaluative, comprehensive literature searches.
- ❑ Distributes library-prepared abstracts of current literature received.
- ❑ Participates as the information resource person on project teams.
- ❑ Arranges for delivery of current information for specific requirements of individual users (for example, uses online database alert systems or wire service filtering software to produce reports tailored to specific individuals in the organization).
- ❑ Has thorough knowledge of subject experts and possible sources of unpublished information in the subject fields of the organization.

ADDITIONAL CONSIDERATIONS

In the preceding checklists no attempt has been made to cover every activity a special librarian performs at the various levels of service. For instance, the area of administration was not covered in the checklists because it is not a direct service function.

The administrative functions of planning, staffing, budgeting, communicating, reporting, evaluating, analyzing, training, coordinating, and so on are performed by special librarians at levels of complexity that relate closely to the levels of service at which the library operates. The success with which the three functions of acquisition, organization, and dissemination are planned and accomplished depends upon the librarian's efficiency as a manager of library operations, as well as upon the level of support the library receives.

Most special libraries are equipped with computers, many of which have direct access to the Internet. Computers greatly simplify the performance of many activities throughout the different levels of function, and may ease the transition from one level of service to the next. In fact, acquiring, organizing, and disseminating information are processes ideally suited for computerization. At least one staff member in a special library should be responsible for keeping the computerized system or systems (e.g. catalog database, World Wide Web pages and links) current and useful.

It is unlikely that any special library would function at a single level of service. A special librarian is far more likely to find that various levels of library services are necessary to meet the information needs of the organization, and to allocate resources to services in light of these requirements. It may be inappropriate in some organizations for the library to function at the maximum levels of service in all its activities, however, for a great many special libraries and their parent organizations, that is the ultimate goal.

The three key functions in a library's operation—acquisition, organization, and dissemination—are each discussed in more detail in the following chapters. The discussion will further illustrate the range of activities in special libraries and suggest how the structured control of information can contribute to the achievement of an organization's goals.

LITERATURE CITED

1. Sharon L. Baker and F. Wilfrid Lancaster, *The Measurement and Evaluation of Library Services*, 2nd ed. (Arlington, VA: Information Resources Press, 1991), 11.

FURTHER READING

Ferne C. Allan. "Benchmarking: Practical Aspects for Information Professionals." *Special Libraries* 84, no.3 (Summer 1993): 123-130.

CHAPTER

5

Where Does the Information Come From?

> *"We are drowning in information but starved for knowledge."*[1]

Among the first steps in organizing a new special library is the acquisition of materials to be used in providing library services. Materials for the new library come from two sources: those already owned by the organization, and new materials to be purchased.

In most organizations there is a great amount of useful material already on hand, but it is often scattered throughout various offices and storage areas, and its existence may be unknown to many of the organization's staff. Further, valuable information arrives unsolicited in the mail and may be scanned by only a few persons before being discarded. The library provides a centralized facility to handle these materials, evaluate their usefulness, and inform appropriate staff of their existence.

New purchases of materials may constitute a substantial portion of the library. To supplement those items already owned, the librarian buys standard materials such as books and periodicals. Computer databases may contain information necessary for accomplishing the library's objectives. Information may also appear in other formats such as technical reports, reprints, pamphlets, newspapers, translations, surveys, clippings, loose-leaf services, microforms, patents, pictures, and government documents. After evaluating materials of all types, those items that meet the library's needs in terms of timeliness, content, and price are selected for inclusion, and orders or subscriptions are placed.

In instances where a previously organized collection exists, many useful materials and procedures may already be in place and some of the steps described below can be modified or eliminated altogether.

MATERIALS ON HAND IN THE ORGANIZATION

Among the important items already owned by an organization are books and periodicals that have been purchased for use in its various departments. In addition, other material useful for reference ordinarily exists within the organization—items such as annual reports, research reports, photographs, financial statements, speeches, memos, and house organs. These items may deal with competing organizations as well as with the organization itself.

Before acquiring new material, it is useful, for reasons of efficiency and economy, to determine what is already on hand. It is important that a record be made of every item so that its location is known to the librarian. While locating existing materials, the librarian becomes familiar with any other deposits of information resources or expertise in the organization. Some may be incorporated into the library but others may not. Often the librarian builds relationships with centers having special knowledge, such as an economic research or legal department, and refers appropriate questions to them for handling. Through the familiarization process, the librarian determines what subscriptions to periodicals and services are in effect and to whom each one goes. Duplication may be discovered that can be eliminated through centralized library ordering and routing of periodicals and services.

It is important that the librarian have the wholehearted cooperation of top management for this task, as some staff members may be reluctant to relinquish physical possession of materials. While it is not essential that every item be moved to the library, materials of value to many employees should be made easily available to them in the library. With existing collections, it is expected that the librarian will exercise caution in discarding items that may have future value. These materials should be set aside for later review when experience will prove or disprove their worth.

MATERIAL TO BE ACQUIRED

It is important to plan with management what the scope of the library will be before adding new materials to the collection. It may not be possible initially to exactly define the scope of the library's interests, the areas to be covered, or the degree of coverage required. In general, it can be assumed that an organization will want to collect information essential to its present and future programs, and that the library will attempt to acquire information that could reasonably be asked for by staff members.

The selection policy of the library is a natural extension of the decisions that have been made regarding the library's scope. The selection policy outlines the depth and extent of coverage of each subject area. It may be decided, for example, that only basic materials will be acquired for business management topics, while subjects relating to the organization's basic products or services will receive in-depth, extensive coverage. Other libraries may find it appropriate to concentrate on highly technical subjects to support the organization's research and product development, while touching only lightly on a narrow range of other subjects.

In addition to the familiar print materials, attention is given to information sources in other formats. Most special libraries find it necessary to obtain information on microfilm or microfiche, in audiovisual forms, and from computer databases. Microfilm and microfiche have become standard items in many special libraries. They offer advantages of space conservation and document preservation, and an increasing amount of material is available in these formats. Materials such as cassette and tape recordings, video tapes, movie films, filmstrips, and the equipment necessary for using them are often included in a special library's collection.

Computers have become standard equipment for most special libraries. They offer access to a large and ever-increasing volume of information on almost every subject. Online databases, available through telecommunications systems from commercial vendors, provide bibliographic citations, abstracts of printed works, or full text of articles and reports. Another computer-based format is CD-ROM (Compact Disc-Read Only Memory). Discs purchased or leased from vendors contain a large volume of data that can be searched with no per use cost or telecommunications charges. When the selection policy for a new library is being formed, it is important to ascertain whether access to information in these formats might reduce the need for purchasing some materials in print format.

INTERLIBRARY LOAN AND DOCUMENT DELIVERY

By their nature special libraries are limited in what they can provide from their own collections, and the "information explosion" of the past decade has made it impossible for even the largest libraries to contain all the materials they may need. Since special libraries cover only one or a few subject fields completely, it is important for special librarians to cooperate with each other and with other libraries in establishing mutually beneficial interlibrary borrowing and lending agreements.

Frequently, special librarians borrow from and lend to each other on an informal basis, using the telephone, messenger services, fax, or the mail to request and receive materials. In many parts of the country, librarians have formed local, regional, and statewide organizations that are designed to foster the sharing of library resources and to encourage improvements in library services. These library organizations often identify existing library resources and provide access to them through cooperative agreements. It is through these cooperative networks, as well as the librarian's personal knowledge of other libraries, that the special librarian is often able to receive nonproprietary information—sometimes even from competing firms or organizations—that would otherwise be difficult or impossible to obtain.

When borrowing from public, academic, and larger special libraries where formal control of materials must be maintained, more formal protocols and paperwork are necessary. The American Library Association's National Interlibrary Loan Code of 1993 sets out the policies and procedures for borrowing formally from these organizations.[2]

Document delivery services are sometimes the easiest way to obtain hard-to-find technical reports, conference proceedings, and articles from obscure journals. Some libraries may even use a *just-in-time* approach to information delivery, where the warehousing of physical collections is kept to a minimum and items are ordered as needed from online vendors or document delivery services. A common practice is for the special library to establish a deposit account with the service against which charges are levied as materials are located and delivered. More libraries are also turning to document delivery services to fulfill document requests due to the increased enforcement of copyright. There is a per copy fee involved in using these services but copyright costs are included. Another way to observe copyright compliance is by subscribing to the Copyright Clearance Center, a service that has a collective licensing system that provides lawful photocopy access to thousands of titles.

ACQUISITIONS

Books, which form the main part of other types of library collections, may be the smallest part of a special library. The collection will often contain only basic texts in the subject field and reference books. In order to build and expand the collection, a librarian uses aids to book selection such as bibliographies and reviews. Trade and professional journals are often the most useful sources of information and are scanned regularly by the librarian for announcements and reviews of new publications. Book publishers' catalogs and advertisements are additional sources of information. For most fields of knowledge, bibliographies of standard, reliable sources of information exist and these bibliographies may suggest items that should be added to the library.

Periodicals often make up a larger proportion of a special library's collection. The proliferation of new periodicals in almost every field makes it necessary to select wisely, and personal examination of a sample issue is the best way to determine what is useful. Most publishers of periodicals will send, without charge, a recent issue of a periodical for examination and review. Older, established periodicals will have been reviewed widely and included in bibliographies or other standard selection aids.

Acquiring books and periodicals directly from the publisher is not difficult; however, the paperwork involved in ordering, receiving, and paying for dozens or even hundreds of individual items is extremely time-consuming. For this reason, many libraries choose to have book orders or subscriptions to periodicals handled by agencies or *jobbers*. Book jobbers will accept and fill orders for books and bill monthly. Ordering through a periodical jobber allows subscriptions to be handled on an annual basis with a common expiration date, reducing clerical work and expense both for the library and the accounting staff. The librarian may choose to order foreign periodicals, as well as books, through a foreign agent or importer rather than directly from the publisher, thus eliminating the problem of foreign monetary exchange and wisely making use of the agent's knowledge of sources.

Government documents are more difficult to obtain, but these items can be of great importance. Many libraries establish a deposit account with the U.S. Government Printing Office and other government agencies against which orders for federal documents are charged. Other libraries use a jobber that specializes in government documents. In some large cities there are U.S. Government Book Stores where some documents may be purchased over the counter. Documents of foreign governments, United Nations documents, and state and local government documents are ordered from the issuing governmental body, or from agencies that contract to distribute them. More and more government information has become available via the Internet, most of it free.

Technical reports play a significant role in many special library collections. Their value, which is largely due to the timeliness of the technical information they contain, decreases rapidly as new developments occur. The librarian's job is to select the reports that are pertinent to the needs of the organization, to announce their availability promptly, and to supply copies as quickly as possible.

Many special libraries use online databases to acquire information as needed. A large variety of databases are offered by vendors such as DIALOG or Dow Jones News/Retrieval. Hundreds of database files containing millions of articles and statistics exist, and more are being created regularly. Charges for gaining access to the databases vary, but many organizations view the costs involved as being reasonable given the wide range of information available, its timeliness, and the speed with which it can be accessed. Charges may include a sign-on fee, a per-hour or per-minute access charge, telecommunications charges, search statement charges, and online and off-line print charges. Training of library personnel to search complex database structures efficiently is offered by vendors at training seminars, often for a fee. Basic equipment needed for computerized databases include a personal computer or end user workstation, a printer, a modem, and appropriate software or shared access to them via a local area network (LAN).

Databases on CD-ROM are another valuable tool for information retrieval. CD-ROM databases offer unlimited use by personnel within the organization, and are often available on disc before printed versions, but not as quickly as online data. CD-ROM discs are purchased or leased for a yearly fee from vendors; many are updated annually, quarterly or more frequently, depending on the nature of the information in the database.

Another way in which librarians are employing leading edge technologies is to filter and deliver information to the users desktop, developing "desktop libraries" by using services such as NewsEDGE, NewsWatch, and Paracel. These services provide users with information directly from a variety of wire services and other timely sources, filtered according to their individual needs and delivered via a user-friendly interface, allowing them to get basic, routine information for themselves, freeing the librarian's time for more specialized in-depth research.

In addition to providing access to external information, computers can handle many clerical tasks involved in purchasing information. Acquisition records can be stored in the computer and orders can be placed using the modem or fax. Records for ordering, receipt, and routing of periodicals are often computer-based. In many special libraries traditional card catalogs have been replaced by computer-based catalogs.

A great deal of free material is available in almost every field, and the librarian looks for such items of interest to the organization. Trade literature forms an important segment of many library collections and is often obtained without charge from associations of which the organization is a member.

CENTRALIZED ORDERING AS A LIBRARY FUNCTION

It can be advantageous to establish the library as the centralized department for handling all of the organization's purchases of books, peri odicals, databases, and other information-related materials. Many information providers offer significant group or volume discounts on their products when the contract is managed by one department. Establishing this as organizational policy results in both economy and speed, and avoids duplication of purchases. The library, through its records, will know who has purchased what and where it is being kept.

If possible, the librarian should establish procedures with the purchasing department whereby the library places its orders for publications directly with vendors. In the case of materials that are needed immediately, orders must often be placed by phone, and the librarian requires the authority to issue them. The librarian should be given the authority to approve all purchases, within reason, in order to facilitate acquisitions with a minimum of delay. Establishing a checking account or credit card for the library may ease and speed purchases. Such practices speed the acquisition process and relieve the purchasing department of considerable paperwork.

LITERATURE CITED

1. John Naisbitt, *Megatrends: Ten New Directions Transforming Our Lives* (New York: Warner Books, 1982), 24.

2. "National Interlibrary Loan Code 1993," *RQ* 33, no. 4 (Summer 1994), 477-479.

FURTHER READING

Gasaway, Laura, and Sarah K. Wiant. *Libraries and Copyright: A Guide to Copyright Law in the 1990s*. Washington, DC: Special Libraries Association, 1994.

CHAPTER

6

How Is the Information Organized?

"Without librarians, we would find ourselves buried under a literal avalanche of totally unorganized, duplicative, and often useless flow of information."[1]

As resources are acquired and assembled in the special library, they must be organized. An effective arrangement of resources and materials assures that users can find information in the library with a minimum of time and effort.

Special librarians possess a broad knowledge of information organizing principles and methods, and bring adaptability and flexibility to the task. Special librarians seek to use simple, easily understood, inexpensive methods where possible, yet they also undertake the development of sophisticated, specialized subject organization schemes when required.

The culture of the organization served by the library must be taken into account when organizing library materials and resources. Specialized populations have specialized information needs. The scheme the special librarian uses for organizing library materials and related finding aids such as card catalogs, indexes, signs, etc. must make sense to the population the library serves.

This chapter discusses the factors involved in organizing library collections and the procedures followed in most special libraries. The physical organization of the collection is discussed in the first section below. Basic tools for identifying and locating specific items are discussed in the second section. Subject analysis methods are explained in the third section. Space requirements for the library collection are a key factor in organization, and are discussed in detail in Chapter 9.

HOUSING AND ARRANGEMENT OF THE COLLECTION

The kinds of shelves, cabinets, and computers used in the library and the physical arrangement of the materials and resources within them are determined by what major types of materials are included in the collection, as well as by considerations of accessibility, convenience, and economy.

Book collections are typically arranged on shelves according to the classification scheme adopted for the special library. Other materials such as video tapes may also be integrated into the shelved book collection. For small collections (300 to 400 titles), a special librarian may find that a simple arrangement of books by author, or by author within broad subject categories, is adequate. For larger collections, a special librarian may need to use a classification scheme that incorporates subject analysis. Such schemes are discussed later in this chapter.

Periodicals (magazines, journals, and newspapers) typically form a large portion of a special library's collection, and are usually arranged alphabetically by title, but sometimes by issuing agency. For example, a bank library might shelve or file all materials from the American Bankers Association together. Current and back issues of periodicals may be kept together in the same section of the library, or current issues may be displayed separately in a reading area. The length of time a periodical title is kept in the library, and whether older issues will be bound or replaced by microforms or computerized storage media, must be determined by the special librarian according to the needs of the organization.

Other materials such as pamphlets, reports, and audio or video tapes, present varying possibilities for arrangement within the library space. The special librarian will determine how best to provide easy access to the materials, based upon both patterns of use and elements intrinsic to the materials themselves, such as size or storage requirements (for example, CD-ROMs must be kept in dust-proof containers). These materials may be arranged by subject, by name or report number of the issuing agency, or by material type. Some individual items or series may be best housed with the book collection. Others may require special cabinets or other storage space constructed for sensitive materials.

At least one computer workstation should be available in the library for searching computerized resources such as CD-ROM products, the Internet, and the catalog, if it is automated. Whether the workstation is used by the library staff to respond to users' information requests, or by users themselves doing independent research, it should be located in a quieter area away from the reference desk, telephone, and traffic through the library. In most organizations, the special librarian searches computer resources for the users, often with the user participating in the process of focusing a search query. Where frequency and intensity of use indicate, the librarian may want to arrange direct access to internal and external databases from users' own desktops or departments.

RECORDS TO IDENTIFY LIBRARY MATERIALS

The library staff creates records of the library's collection. Traditionally, this set of records is maintained in a printed card catalog, but the catalog may not be in card form at all; it may be a printed book catalog, or it may be an online catalog existing only in electronic records accessible via computer workstations. All types of library catalog records provide information about the author, title, and general subject content of an item in the library collection, and a classification number or code for locating each item.

Some special libraries have professional staff members who create catalog records of the resources in the collection. This is useful if the library collection includes many materials specific to the parent organization. Catalog records for published resources are available from various suppliers. Some libraries purchase printed catalog cards from cataloging sources such as a library system's headquarters. Other special libraries subscribe to the services of computerized bibliographic networks such as OCLC, the Online Computer Library Center in Ohio, which offer access to a pool of cataloging records from other libraries, and usually provide tapes or cards of the member libraries' records to them. In-depth cataloging is most commonly done or obtained for the books in a special library's collection, but not for resources in the other formats mentioned above.

The special librarian also needs to provide users with some basic listing of the periodical collection. The same records can be used by library staff for processing periodicals. Many special libraries maintain a card or computer file that contains receipt records for each periodical title and issue, subscription records, routing information, and policies for retention of back issues. Computer software used for these purposes usually has the ability to create a list or file of holdings for reference by library users.

Permanent records may not be needed for some of the library's materials. The special librarian will determine this based on users' information needs and the organization's record retention policies, if relevant. Short-lived materials such as preprints (copies of articles distributed prior to publication) can be indexed or abstracted quickly for immediate, short-term use. Ephemeral items such as news clippings, advertising pieces and pamphlets can be cataloged in an abbreviated format in the main catalog, or simply arranged in subject files.

After considering the computer equipment available within the organization, requirements for effective services, and comparative costs, the special librarian implements the most efficient method of creating records that help users identify and locate the library's holdings. Preparation of catalogs and other finding aids is a vital part of library work, and ensures that users have easy access to the collection. This function is one in which the use of computers may result in more effective records at a lower cost than the use of manual methods.

SUBJECT ANALYSIS

Classification, subject cataloging, and indexing are three major ways of providing subject access to information. Each of these will be explained briefly below, since decisions on the amount of subject analysis performed influence the capacity of the library to provide information service and the cost of operating the library. Information professionals may need to use a blend of these three methods to best provide their users subject access to the library collection. In some cases, two types of subject analysis are applied to each item. For example, most university libraries classify books (assign them a call number that represents a subject area) and catalog them (assign them one or more terms from a controlled vocabulary). The extent of subject analysis work done in a particular library is determined by the organization's requirements for in-depth coverage by subject and the speed of document recovery needed for each type of material.

CLASSIFICATION

Classification systems organize knowledge in logical groupings of related subjects. Call numbers are derived from classification systems. These systems are generally used for both arranging materials in libraries and for arranging entries in bibliographies, indexes, and abstracting services. There are four general approaches to classifying materials.

- Using an established general classification, such as the Dewey Decimal System or the Library of Congress Classification System.
- Using a specialized system for a particular subject area.
- Adaptating one of these general or specialized systems.
- Creating an original classification system tailored to a particular collection.

The culture and vocabulary of the library's users, the nature of the library's materials, and the size of the collection are the major factors the special librarian considers in determining which classification system to use. The following are examples of instances in which various classification systems could be used.

- The Dewey Decimal System works well for classifying materials in libraries that cover a wide range of subjects, none of them in great depth.
- The Library of Congress Classification System is very expandable and so is useful for libraries collecting materials in great depth on a few subjects.
- The Physics and Astronomy Classification Scheme (PACS) is an example of a specialized system covering subject matter in physics and astronomy using hierarchically arranged terms; it would work well in an observatory library.

Classification schemes are often more useful to library staff for organizing materials than for people using the materials in the collection.

The casual library user rarely wants to learn the complexities of a classification system. If the library is open 24 hours a day (often the case in medical facilities, for example), or if the library's online catalog is accessible 24 hours a day, the special librarian can best aid users in finding materials for themselves by employing well-defined subject terms in the catalog records, with classification numbers having less importance.

SUBJECT CATALOGING

Subject cataloging is the process of selecting appropriate subject terms or headings to reflect and sometimes describe the content of each item cataloged. The term *subject heading* is often used because subject terms are listed at the top of cards in a printed catalog, or on folders containing filed materials. Subject terms are also used for keyword searches in many library online catalogs.

In order to achieve consistency and effectiveness in cataloging, an information professional uses a limited subject heading list or thesaurus for selecting subject terms, thus eliminating redundant headings. Such controlled vocabulary ensures uniformity and assists the library staff, as well as the library users, in identifying keywords that describe needed information. Special librarians often use basic lists such as the *Library of Congress Subject Headings* or *Sears List of Subject Headings*, sometimes with modifications to suit the particular library. As in the case of classification schemes, a wide array of subject heading lists are used by special librarians. Some examples of specialized lists or thesauri follow.

- *Medical Subject Headings, Annotated Alphabetic List* (Annotated MeSH)
- *Moys Classification and Thesaurus for Legal Materials*
- *Musaurus, A New Approach to Organising Music Information*
- *NASA Thesaurus*
- *Thesaurus of Psychological Index Terms*

Subject cataloging requires time and funds, and so is typically done only for the materials that will form the permanent portion of the library's collection. In deciding which materials should be cataloged, the special librarian determines how long items will be retained in the library, how important they are to potential users, and whether subject access would be used by people to find these materials in the collection. It is seldom necessary to classify or catalog in any detail ephemeral materials that will be discarded or replaced in a few months, so these may simply be organized by subject and placed in alphabetically arranged files.

The Internet has introduced a new element to library cataloging. Some special librarians catalog selected pages on the World Wide Web, most often the organization's or the library's own pages, which are expected to remain useful for a long time. Web resources for specific projects and other short-lived uses can be linked to the library's homepage for the duration, but it should not be necessary to catalog them.

INDEXING

Indexing analyzes the contents of materials in greater depth than simple subject cataloging. Indexing usually involves preparing card files, lists, or databases containing references to topics, names, and other key elements in books, periodicals, reports, patents, and other materials. Special librarians often prepare a summary, or abstract, of the content of the document in conjunction with indexing the item. The amount of indexing done within a special library depends largely upon the availability and suitability of commercially produced indexes.

The cost of in-house indexing and abstracting and the needs of the organization are the criteria the special librarian weighs against subscribing to commercial indexing services. Printed periodical indexes, such as *The Business Periodical Index*, are purchased by many special libraries, and used both by staff for indexing tools, and by users for finding aids. Many such topical indexes are also available in CD-ROM format, via online services or on the Internet. There are also many less-well-known indexes, both printed and computer-based, in specialized subject areas. One such example is INSPEC, which indexes published articles and conference proceedings in the fields of physics, engineering, and computer sciences.

In addition to controlled vocabulary indexing systems that use subject heading lists, there are systems in use which rely on natural language as used in a document. UNITERM is one such system, developed by Mortimer Taube to index the vast amount of scientific and technical literature from World War II.[2] Two other widely used natural language index systems are KWIC (Key Word In Context) and KWOC (Key Word Out of Context).[3]

Special librarians may also prepare indexes for internal materials such as executive committee minutes, confidential company data, house newsletters, or annual reports. These indexes can be a valuable key to information that would otherwise be filed away or lost. Because of their special knowledge of subject analysis systems and techniques, special librarians may also be asked to help members of the organization arrange information files, or recommend indexing systems or software for electronic files.

LITERATURE CITED

1. William O. Dannhousend, Publisher's Comments, *Better Roads* 66, no. 4 (April 1996): 8.
2. Mortimer Taube and Associates, *Studies in Coordinate Indexing* (Washington, DC: Documentation Inc., 1953).
3. Phillip McDonald, "Free-Language Indexes," *Literature of Science* (Brisbane: Griffith University Library Reference Department, 1995). Available from http://medea.itc.gu.edu.au/reference/litsci/ abstract.htm; accessed 13 December 1996.

FURTHER READING

American Institute of Physics. *Physics and Astronomy Classification Scheme: PACS.* New York: American Institute of Physics.

Business Periodicals Index. New York, NY: H. W. Wilson Company.

Dewey, Melvil. *Dewey Decimal Classification and Relative Index*, 20th ed. Dublin, OH: OCLC Forest Press, 1989.

Institute of Electrical Engineers. *Information Services in Physics, Electrotechnology, Computers and Control (INSPEC).* London: Institute of Electrical Engineers.

Library of Congress. *Library of Congress Classification Schedules.* Detroit: Gale Research.

Library of Congress Subject Headings, 19th ed. Washington, DC: Library of Congress, 1996.

McDonald, Phillip. *Literature of Science: Free-Language Indexes.* Brisbane: Griffith University Library Reference Department, 1995.

Medical Subject Headings, Annotated Alphabetic List (Annotated MeSH). Bethesda: National Library of Medicine, 1995.

Moys, Elizabeth M. *Moys Classification and Thesaurus for Legal Materials.* London: Bowker-Saur, 1992.

Musaurus, A Music Thesaurus: A New Approach to Organising Music Information. London: Music Press, 1991.

NASA Thesaurus. Washington, DC: National Aeronautics and Space Administration, Scientific and Technical Branch, 1994.

Readers' Guide to Periodical Literature. New York: H. W. Wilson Co.

Sears, Minnie Earl. *Sears List of Subject Headings,* 15th ed. Edited by Joseph Miller. New York: H. W. Wilson Co., 1994.

Subject Analysis Systems (SAS) Collection. University of Toronto, Faculty of Information Studies Library.

Taube, Mortimer and Associates. *Studies in Coordinate Indexing.* Washington, DC: Documentation Incorporated, 1953.

Walker, Alvin, Jr., ed. *Thesaurus of Psychological Index Terms.* Washington, DC: American Psychological Association, 1994.

CHAPTER

7

How Does the Information Get to the User?

". . . librarians are more than technicians. They are, it seems, information therapists who analyze problems as well as find answers."[1]

The most vital service the special library performs is delivering information to users. Providing essential information in support of the organization's goals is the reason the library exists. The activities of acquiring and organizing information discussed in the previous chapters support this dissemination function.

The major efforts of the library and the librarian are focused on getting information as quickly and efficiently as possible into the hands of employees who need it. The value of special librarians is often measured by their ability to accurately and effectively respond to their users' needs, which may range from keeping current on developments in a particular field to becoming educated in an unfamiliar subject area to the need for a telephone number. Common ways of providing effective information dissemination services to users are described in this chapter.

REFERENCE SERVICES

Reference service is the most well-known dissemination technique the special library provides; it is basic to the operation of all libraries. It is often the most effective means of answering the many questions that arise each day because the librarian is well trained in the research techniques necessary to locate the best information in the least time at the lowest cost.

At a minimum level of reference service, the librarian maintains a collection of necessary reference books, locates basic factual answers, directs users to sources in the library, and identifies and obtains additional information resources from other locations inside and outside the organization. In this scenario the librarian guides the users through their own research.

At a maximum level of reference service, the librarian does the research, freeing the valuable time of the user. This requires the librarian to have a thorough knowledge of the subject field and the literature available, the guides to the literature, and organizations and individuals doing research in the field. This level of service ranges from answering a simple question to an exhaustive search of the literature on a subject. And, through a familiarity with the library's users and their interests, the librarian can plan for the organization's needs and provide pertinent materials before they are requested. Service at this level requires a staff of librarians with more time, knowledge, responsibility, and clerical support.

One of the main challenges facing the special library is the need to balance the use of personnel resources between acquiring and organizing the library's materials and disseminating information to the organization's users. Management and library staff must work together to ensure that the library's workload is maintained at a level that enables the librarian to focus on helping the users find the information they need. The advantage of having a trained librarian on staff is his/her expertise in determining which resources—print, online, or personal—are most productive, and the logical, methodical, comprehensive research techniques they employ to answer questions.

The librarian also brings expertise in determining a user's exact information needs. Often users approach librarians with a seemingly simple question, but do not communicate their real need. A good reference librarian conducts a reference interview to ensure understanding of the underlying need and how the information will be used. Employing this reference process enables them to act as effective intermediaries in performing the research to obtain a satisfactory answer to the real question. The basic steps of the reference process are as follows.

1. Focus the question through the reference interview.
2. Identify and select appropriate sources.
3. Perform the search.
4. Package the information concisely.
5. Present the requester with the answer.

The answer may be as simple as the name, address, and telephone number of a company taken from a directory; or it may result in many pages of text and statistics located through searching computer databases, checking indexes, reading abstracts, and making full use of the resources available.

CURRENT AWARENESS SERVICES

Current awareness services range from automated desktop delivery systems to more traditional methods such as acquisition lists and bulletins produced by the library. With the continuing expansion of information resources, users may need to receive ongoing, up-to-date information on topics of interest to them delivered directly to their workstation. Many commercial information services provide these types of services. The librarian works with these vendors and library users to select services appropriate to the information needs of the organization. Once such a service is in place, the librarian works with users to select and refine filters or search profiles to ensure that the most relevant information reaches them.

If a desktop delivery service is not appropriate, the librarian can provide a number of other current awareness services. Sometimes referred to as SDI, or selective dissemination of information, this type of service updates a library user on a research topic each business day or less frequently, depending upon their needs. Many commercial online vendors provide a means to produce search results automatically that can easily be passed on to users at differing intervals.

New resources available in the library can be announced to potential users in regularly issued acquisition lists and bulletins through either print or electronic mail, or via a database that is updated and can be accessed by anyone in the company. These tools keep all users aware of new resources available in the library. Annotations or abstracts are sometimes provided in order to give a better guide to the contents of articles, books, and pamphlets.

Commercial services are available in many subject areas to keep users up-to-date with the literature in a specific field. The service provides listings of pertinent material, abstracts, and copies of documents or articles. Users want to see these listings regularly to select needed material for themselves or their departments. Librarians also utilize these services as an aid to selecting and ordering materials for future reference work.

In many organizations the library staff scans literature as it arrives. They then distribute listings or relevant references on subjects such as newly approved patents, new products, competitive intelligence, or research in progress to users with an ongoing interest in the information. This, however, is a labor-intensive technique and may be complimented by computerized updating services.

ROUTING SERVICES

Routing services take several forms. At a minimum level of service, periodicals or tables of contents are physically routed to employees. At a maximum level, librarians provide staff with critical bibliographies and abstracts of current literature received. Whichever method is used, the purpose is the same—the information needs to be disseminated to the users for it to be effective.

When periodicals arrive in the library, their receipt is recorded and they are made available to readers, usually on the same day. Routing involves either attaching a list of names to the periodical's cover and distributing it through interoffice mail or, in smaller organizations, passing it from person to person. In libraries where periodical check-in is automated, routing lists are generally produced by the computer when the item is checked in. When routing lists are long, multiple subscriptions to a title may be necessary to achieve timely distribution.

In some large organizations, the most effective way to give library users an opportunity to see the contents of a single subscription to a periodical is to keep it in the library. Displaying current periodicals makes it easy for users to come into the library and scan them, giving all users equal access to the newest printed information. When a periodical is of immediate interest to only a few people, it can be sent directly to their attention and later displayed in the library.

In some libraries it has been a practice to photocopy tables of contents of newly arrived periodicals for distribution to inform employees of new articles available. Interested readers are then sent copies of articles at their request. This practice may be a violation of copyright law. Likewise, photocopying newsletters for routing or distribution is a violation of copyright. Commercial services are available that will provide tables of contents directly to the users via e-mail and allow articles to be ordered directly, charging an appropriate copyright fee.

The 1992 landmark decision of *American Geophysical Union vs. Texaco* "ruled that commercial companies which make copies of copyrighted articles published in scientific and technical journals violate fair use under the Copyright Act of 1976."[2] Because of this decision, many libraries register with the Copyright Clearance Center (CCC), which facilitates the payment of appropriate royalties to the copyright holder of works registered with the CCC.[3] It is important to note, however, that not every publication is registered with the CCC.

USE OF OUTSIDE SOURCES OF INFORMATION

Because their collections are so narrowly focused, special librarians regularly use sources of information from outside the organization as a part of their problem-solving, information-gathering function. When handling a request for information on a new or unfamiliar topic—one that is beyond the scope of the organization's collection—the librarian knows how to locate people outside the organization who can assist in locating authoritative information on such subjects. This assistance may be in the form of access to other librarians or specialists through telephone calls, correspondence, or visits; arranging user access to other libraries and information centers; interlibrary borrowing; or contracting with information brokers or document delivery services.

Special librarians have a tradition of borrowing materials informally from one another based on professional relationships and personal acquaintance. Through this informal network materials are obtained quickly and with a minimum of paperwork, often as a result of a single phone call. Developing these contacts through attending local and national meeting of professional groups is important. The time spent networking is well spent when a professional colleague has the expertise and resources to provide information that would have taken longer to obtain via other channels. Another special librarian will also recognize and appreciate the timely manner in which information is required and be more willing to provide a quick answer to a request.

The Internet has become a networking tool for librarians. Mailing lists are often the most efficient means of doing this. By subscribing to a mailing list that focuses on reference work, business libraries, or any number of other special topics, a librarian has immediate access to the expertise of like-minded information professionals worldwide. A difficult request posted to the list in the morning might be answered that afternoon by another librarian on the other side of the world who has that specific information.

Formal interlibrary cooperation groups have been formed by special, public, academic, and school libraries in many regions. These groups have developed their own policies and regulations regarding interlibrary loan and other cooperative programs. They often publish directories and guides to the use of each others libraries, combined listings of periodical holdings, and other mutually beneficial tools. As special libraries gain experience with these regional cooperative networks, they discover new sources of nearby, accessible information beneficial to their organizations, and they reciprocate by making materials in their libraries available to outside users who have a need for the information in their collections.

The local public library as well as college and university libraries are also excellent sources for a wide range of information, but one should remember that their first responsibility is to their own pool of users and their policies for use may be restrictive. Some public libraries and universities have departments that provide research service on a contract basis or for an established fee.

Some research organizations and commercial vendors undertake special research projects on a fee basis. Special librarians also seek information from associations, public relations offices, foreign embassies and consulates, public officials, governmental agencies, and scholars at universities, museums, and research organizations. Using outside sources and services should not be used as a substitute for collecting needed information or providing adequate reference services, but as a legitimate extension of dealing with vast amounts of published and unpublished information, some of it in unfamiliar areas.

OTHER LIBRARY SERVICES

A number of other services dealing with managing information may fall within the scope of the librarian's responsibilities.

KNOWLEDGE MANAGEMENT

Many concepts traditionally associated with libraries are more broadly applied to the emerging concept of corporate knowledge management.[4] The librarian has the expertise to create, maintain, and retrieve data from those formal or informal documents that make up an organization's intellectual capital. Knowledge databases, or knowledgebases, often utilize workgroup software, such as Lotus Notes, which is also used for library applications. The librarian's participation as an integral part of the teams within the organization makes him/her a logical choice to act as knowledge manager. Often combining internal information with retrieval of external information is advantageous to the organization's mission and goals.

ABSTRACTS

In some special libraries, providing abstracts of information is an important activity. Abstracts are summaries of larger works that outline their contents and can be read quickly to determine the need to read the entire work. Abstracts can be used in libraries as elements of the current awareness service and, because of their succinct language, they are easily indexed.

TRANSLATIONS

From time to time articles of importance are written in foreign languages and translations are needed. The librarian can locate a commercial translator or translating agency to provide these translations. Possibly the library staff may be able to undertake the work, depending on its language fluencies. Before deciding upon original translation, the librarian determines whether the document has already been translated and if a copy of the translation is available. The National Translations Center at the Library of Congress serves as the U.S. depository and information clearinghouse on unpublished translations. Several hundred thousand translations are on file there, received from industry and government agencies internationally.

ARCHIVES

Archives, those documents relating to the growth and development of an organization, are often placed within the jurisdiction of the special library. The special librarian preserves materials by collecting, classifying, and indexing those items of potential historical value. Because of its age and fragility, this material often requires special handling and storage facilities. Organizations having archives view them with great pride and may find them increasingly useful.

DOCUMENT MANAGEMENT

The enormous number of internal documents resulting from the activities of an organization may be retained for future use or for legal reasons. These internally produced documents may be kept in the library as a part of the organization's working collection of materials, or they may be organized as a separate entity. Document management may be included as part of the overall responsibility of knowledge management, or it may be considered a separate function. Assigning responsibility for document management to the library should occur at the maximum level of function with sufficient additional staff.

MARKETING THE LIBRARY

Although good information service is the best public relations for a special library, both management and the library should be sure that employees are kept aware of how the library can help them in their work. Even at a minimum level of function, it is important to encourage employees to use the information resources that the organization is providing for them.

INVOLVEMENT IN ORGANIZATIONAL EVENTS

Depending on the organization, there may be sponsored events or high profile projects where library involvement would be appropriate and beneficial to both the library and the organization's employees. Library staff may give presentations at staff meetings, tailoring explanations of library services to the particular needs of each audience. Webpages and participation in the organization's intranet also raise the visibility of the library. Some libraries have organized regular Internet "user group" meetings, for instance a monthly brown bag lunch session, to promote sharing of knowledge and experience with the Internet. Every effort should be made to include library staff in any of the organization's activities that provide opportunities for marketing information services to users.

LIBRARY BROCHURES

Many special libraries prepare brochures describing the library's resources and services. This technique of promoting the library and its services is a valuable reminder to the organization's employees of the availability of information resources, and can also be used as a public relations or informational piece for distribution to persons outside the organization. The library's current awareness bulletins, newsletters, and other publications are also effective ways to publicize library services.

LIBRARY ORIENTATION

Ideally, new employees should attend orientation sessions after they have had enough time to understand what their new jobs entail and how the library could contribute to their success. The librarian ensures that the library's brochure and other publications are available to new employee, then, after an appropriate time, initiates a more in-depth orientation session. Generally, this session consists of a tour of the library facility, location, and discussion of resources available in various subject areas, and a description of the services offered. This is a good time to make certain that the employee's name is included on appropriate periodical routing lists, to identify potential topics for current awareness services, and to schedule any training sessions for searching computer databases.

USER TRAINING

The special librarian is often responsible for scheduling or performing training activities for employees who need to be able to search online databases or use news filtering services. This activity involves scheduling time at the computer, scheduling internal or outside training sessions, assisting users who are having difficulty or need extra help, and tracking time and charges.

Common problems associated with end user searching are that once trained, users often lose their enthusiasm for the process, don't keep up with the changes in the system, or forget search techniques because they conduct searches infrequently. For this reason, many special librarians find it useful to exercise some control over end user searching, performing searches jointly with the user or doing the search for the user.

To obtain maximum benefit and effectiveness from a library operation, information must flow to the library as well as from the library. The librarian should be informed of changes and new developments in the organization's projects, programs, and goals, so that library services remain focused on those goals, and so staff have sufficient warning to develop any new resources or services required to meet them. A direct alliance between the librarian and a high-ranking executive is beneficial in keeping the library positioned at the center of the organization's information needs.

LITERATURE CITED

1. Bonnie A. Nardi, Vicki O'Day, and Edward J. Valauskas, "Put a Good Librarian, Not Software, in Driver's Seat," *The Christian Science Monitor*, 4 June 1996: 18.
2. Laura N. Gasaway and Sarah K. Wiant, *Libraries and Copyright: A Guide to Copyright Law in the 1990s* (Washington, DC: Special Libraries Association, 1994), 44.
3. Ibid., 68.
4. Lenny Liebmann, "Web Servers Foster 'Workflow Without Walls'," *CommunicationsWeek* No. 595 (5 February 1996): 46.

FURTHER READING

"Copyright Act of 1976." 17 *United States Code* 101 et seq.

Gasaway, Laura, and Sarah K. Wiant. *Libraries and Copyright: A Guide to Copyright Law in the 1990s*. Washington, DC: Special Libraries Association, 1994.

CHAPTER

8

Who Staffs the Special Library?

The most critical component in delivering key content services and products is the people—their abilities, their core competencies, the match between these and the corporation's culture, vision and values..."[1]

Efficient and effective library service requires the same careful analysis of personnel requirements and recruitment as is necessary in other units of the organization. The special library usually includes professional and clerical staff. Both professional and clerical staff positions require certain specialized qualifications or capabilities for information service. Members of the library staff are also employees of the parent organization, and compatibility with the organization and the employees they are to serve is also an important consideration.

The first step in building the library staff is to hire the professional librarian to manage the library. The librarian, in conjunction with the organization's personnel unit, is responsible for defining specific jobs, writing job descriptions, determining qualifications, and advising and assisting in the employment process.

PROFESSIONAL STAFF

The capabilities of the special librarian center on three considerations. First, the emphasis on the information function requires a strong commitment to, and active promotion of, information service. Second, the special librarian needs a strong interest in the subject fields necessary for the organization. Third, as manager of the library, the special librarian needs strong management skills. The special librarian is also a member of the professional and managerial staff of the organization and must have the interpersonal skills necessary to interact effectively with the rest of the organization's staff in both service and managerial roles. These characteristics should be kept in mind during the process of recruiting professional personnel for the library.

EDUCATION

Education and experience in both professional librarianship and subject knowledge are important considerations. The special librarian has a professional education—the master of library science or equivalent degree—and should have related library experience. Professional education and experience enable the librarian to gauge accurately, plan correctly, analyze shrewdly, and acquire and organize information and services to the organization's optimum advantage. The special librarian also provides essential expertise in how people use information, and how to effectively communicate it to them.

Professional education in library science also teaches librarians how to obtain a working knowledge of a subject and its information resources and rapidly develop expertise in a subject field. Ideally, the special librarian also possesses education or equivalent experience in the subject areas of concern to the organization, and has a strong desire to keep abreast of new developments across a broad spectrum of interests. In any case, it is important that the special librarian be respected as a professional who understands the organization's interests, and that users have confidence in the information provided.

A point often debated is whether emphasis should be on the subject specialty or on librarianship. In some fields and for some functions a strong subject background, usually provided through an undergraduate degree or experience in the field, is important. For example, pharmaceutical company libraries often require biology, chemistry, or health science backgrounds. Likewise, business and economics backgrounds are valuable specialties in banks and financial institutions and insurance companies. Many libraries seek various specializations so that the professional staff members complement each other in subject background and are capable of handling information over a wide range of subjects. But these are not hard and fast rules. Special librarians often have a liberal arts education that emphasizes broad knowledge coupled with the analytical skills necessary to effectively evaluate and analyze information. The educational or experiential background sought for other employees should also provide valid guidelines in seeking professional library staff.

PERSONAL QUALIFICATIONS

A strong motivation to put knowledge to work is the characteristic that best exemplifies the special librarian. To consider the position as mainly custodial is to lose sight of this key characteristic. While good housekeeping is essential, it is a phase of the work that can be handled by good clerical personnel properly trained and supervised by the librarian. An effective librarian has the interpersonal skills to enter groups easily, generate confidence and trust, and be accepted as a peer in the organization. The librarian must be able to deal with a variety of personalities and problems and establish priorities for competing demands. Other desirable characteristics include perseverance, a sense of intellectual empathy with users and their work while retaining objectivity, and a sincere desire to work with and assist others in furthering the organization's goals. Above all, in considering personal qualifications, it should be kept in mind that the librarian is a member of the professional and managerial staff of the organization and must be accepted by and be able to interact with them.

There are two common pitfalls for organizations seeking a librarian for the first time. The first is hiring a cataloger on the theory that physical organization will solve the organization's information problems. It should be evident by now that the physical collection is only the beginning of information service, that the organization needs someone who can manage information in the organization's culture. Second, while new library school graduates may be desirable candidates, it is also generally wise to hire as experienced a library manager as possible. While a new librarian and a new library can grow together, the experienced library manager brings a wealth of practical knowledge to the situation and is able to establish efficient and effective service more rapidly while avoiding potentially expensive missteps.

PROFESSIONAL SPECIALTIES

As in other professions, librarians can be specialists as well as general practitioners. In a large library operation, technical specialists concentrate on organizing and analyzing information for future retrieval and use: examples include the cataloger, indexer, database expert, records manager, archivist, and systems analyst. Others who are subject specialists may devote most of their time to direct assistance to users: the reference librarians who receive the questions, clarify them, and ferret out the answers; the literature and database searchers and bibliographers who search and compile relevant references; the translator of foreign languages; and the abstractor who analyzes and succinctly presents the basic information in a paragraph or two. Computer technology is a basic part of library operations, and all professional librarians need to know the principal techniques and trends in computer-based information management. Many are familiar with systems analysis and programming. Even more have expertise with bibliographic and reference databases and can work with both computer systems staff and end users in implementing automated systems. The librarian should also be able to use Internet resources and protocols.

In the small library, one professional librarian may perform many or all of these functions and will need to be a generalist. When there are two or more professionals present, they may divide the several operations and their backgrounds may reflect various specialties. These different needs in terms of attributes and skills should be taken into consideration in the search for professional library staff.

RECRUITING

Although many searches for professional librarians are conducted on a local or regional basis, national searches are not uncommon. There are a number of specialized placement sources that can be used to locate professional librarians. Many of these sources are available at little or no cost to either job seeker or employer. Telephone joblines are an excellent source as are library associations and graduate library schools, most of which offer placement services.

The search for a professional librarian may prove more difficult where specific subject qualifications and experience are sought. As an indication of demand, the following list gives 1994 placements by subject specialty in order of frequency.[2]

1. Law
2. Business, finance, and corporate
3. Science and technology
4. Medical
5. Communications industry
6. Non-library information services
7. Historical agencies and archives
8. Databases
9. Art and museum
10. Professional associations

In 1994 the average salary for a new graduate entering a special library in the United States was $28,086. This average starting salary is currently increasing annually by 5 or 6 percent. Salaries of graduates with relevant backgrounds and experience are considerably higher.[3]

The estimated mean for all special librarians as of 1996 was $46,805 in the United States (in U.S. dollars) and $49,107 (in Canadian dollars) in Canada. Salaries vary by geographic region, by type of organization, and by position held in the special library. Table 8-1 shows salaries for various positions as of 1996.[4]

Most graduate library and information science schools provide placement services for past and present graduates. The American Library Association (ALA) is the accrediting agency for library schools in the United States and Canada. The ALA has developed standards for programs of graduate education for librarianship, normally leading to a master's degree. Job descriptions may be submitted to selected schools. A list of graduate library school programs accredited by the ALA can be found in Appendix C.

Professional associations offer a variety of placement services and the various specialized associations are particularly good sources when specific subject expertise is being sought.

TABLE 8-1
SALARIES OF SPECIAL LIBRARIANS BY PRIMARY RESPONSIBILITY

PRIMARY RESPONSIBILITY	MEDIAN	MEAN
UNITED STATES (U.S. Dollars)		
Administrative Responsibility	$55,000	$58,406
Systems Specialist	$43,000	$45,099
Subject Specialist	$42,396	$45,369
Abstractor/Indexer	$36,439	$39,599
Reader Service/Reference	$39,999	$40,369
Literature/Online Searcher	$43,716	$44,914
Acquisitions/Cataloging	$37,433	$39,465
General Responsibility	$40,000	$41,518
CANADA (Canadian Dollars)		
Administrative Responsibility	$55,776	$56,740
Subject Specialist	$45,805	$48,912
Reader Services/Reference	$43,750	$44,387
Literature/Online Searcher	$42,000	$47,972
Acquisitions/Cataloging	$38,400	$39,333
General Responsibility	$45,000	$44,666

Special Libraries Association, *SLA Biennial Salary Survey 1997* (Washington, DC: Special Libraries Association, 1996).

The headquarters of the Special Libraries Association (SLA) maintains a telephone jobline called SpeciaLine, offers a Resume Referral Service for employers and job seekers, carries placement advertising in its periodical, *Information Outlook*, and provides an employment clearinghouse at annual conferences. Many of SLA's local chapters in the United States and Canada offer employment services in their areas through telephone joblines or employment chairpersons. Names of chapter contacts can be obtained from SLA Headquarters in Washington, DC.

The Medical Library Association (MLA) carries placement advertising in the *MLA News* and offers a placement clearinghouse at its annual meeting. The American Association of Law Libraries (AALL) carries job listings in its newsletter and maintains a telephone jobline at its headquarters in Chicago. Some local AALL chapters have placement officers who are available for counseling and referrals. The American Society for Information Science (ASIS) publishes *ASIS Jobline*, a monthly newsletter of employment opportunities, and offers a placement clearinghouse at its annual meetings.

The American Library Association and its various divisions offer a variety of placement resources for all types of libraries, including advertising in ALA and division publications and conference placement services. ALA's Office for Library Personnel Resources (OLPR) publishes a comprehensive *Guide to Library Placement Sources*, available from the OLPR. This guide includes all types of placement sources and is an indispensable resource for both employers and job seekers. It is also published in R. R. Bowker Company's *Library and Book Trade Almanac*, an annual publication available at most public libraries. Addresses for the associations described above are included in Appendix D.

Telephone joblines that carry recorded messages of job openings in a specific geographic region are maintained by many national, state, and local library associations. Although the information is brief, the jobline has the advantage of quick and up-to-date listings at minimal cost. In addition, a few joblines are offered as online databases or through electronic bulletin boards. Specific information and telephone numbers for the joblines are published in the *Guide to Library Placement Sources* described above and are listed in the "Career Leads" section of ALA's monthly *American Libraries*.

Classified as well as display advertising for positions may be placed in a number of professional library periodicals, including.

- *Information Outlook* (SLA), 1700 Eighteenth Street NW, Washington, DC 20009-2508
- *American Libraries* "Career Leads" (ALA), 50 E. Huron Street, Chicago, IL 60611
- *ASIS Jobline* (ASIS), 8760 Georgia Avenue, Suite 501, Silver Springs, MD 20910-3602
- *College & Research Libraries News* (ALA, Association of College and Research Libraries), 50 E. Huron Street, Chicago, IL 60611
- *Library Journal* (Cahners Publishing Company), 249 W. 17th Street, New York, NY 10011
- *Library Hotline* (Cahners Publishing Company), 249 W. 17th Street, New York, NY 10011

Private employment services and search firms specializing in library personnel can be found in some metropolitan areas, and some of these firms operate on a national basis. They are listed in the ALA *Guide to Library Placement Sources* described above, and some advertise in the "ConsultantBase" section published quarterly in *American Libraries*.

As for more general sources, local newspapers also carry library positions, particularly in their Sunday editions. *The New York Times* Sunday "Week in Review" section carries a special section of librarian positions in addition to regular classifieds.

PROFESSIONAL ACTIVITIES

As with other professions, librarians have established professional associations. These associations produce publications of various types for assistance and instruction; hold periodic meetings and conferences that benefit the librarian through programs and personal contacts; sponsor continuing education programs to keep librarians abreast of developing information technologies; serve as a focal point for the library community to respond to matters of regional and national import in library and information service; and provide many different services to members, employers, and their respective communities of interest.

The primary association for special librarians is the Special Libraries Association, which includes subject-oriented divisions such as Business and Finance, Science and Technology, Law, and local or regional chapters. The Medical Library Association, the American Association of Law Libraries, and the Council of Planning Librarians are examples of more specialized groups. The American Library Association serves all types of libraries and library services yet includes units devoted to areas of interest to special librarians. The American Society for Information Science is another group that attracts many special librarians.

There are also professional organizations for various specialties, the Society of American Archivists, the Association of Records Managers and Administrators (ARMA International), the Society of Competitive Intelligence Professionals, to name a few (see Appendix D).

Many special librarians also belong to and participate in other groups related to their subject specialties, such as the American Chemical Society, the Technical Association of the Paper and Pulp Industry, the American Marketing Association, the American Management Association, and other scientific, business, and technical associations.

SUPPORT STAFF

The daily functioning of most libraries requires some amount of clerical and routine work, such as receipt and routing of publications, typing, word processing and data entry, filing, clipping, record keeping, ordering, and processing. An organization may employ a clerk or secretary for these chores, assign the *librarian* title, and proclaim itself well served, but these are just custodial functions. Good information service begins with a professional librarian planning and supervising the performance of clerical and support work and using the results as tools in achieving the library's more extensive goals. It is essential that the professional librarian be provided with competent assistance, otherwise, information service will be limited to routine tasks, and the opportunity for active contribution to the organization will be lost. The importance of adequate clerical support cannot be overstated.

Local sources for support personnel are much the same as for similar positions elsewhere in the organization, although in some areas joblines and library personnel employment agencies are also available for support positions.

In many respects, support positions in the organization's library correspond to clerical, secretarial, or general assistant positions elsewhere in the organization. While most support staff train on the job for library work, sometimes certain expertise is needed and the library will seek a paraprofessional. Community colleges in many areas offer courses dealing with some of the basic techniques of library operation, such as acquisitions procedures, circulation records control, and simple reference and cataloging. Graduates of these programs are known as library technical assistants (LTAs) and they constitute a subprofessional grade level between basic clerical staff and the professional librarian. LTAs can perform a very useful function in relieving professional staff from relatively routine tasks. They are not, however, intended to substitute for professional staff, nor does their limited training prepare them for such appointments.

Qualities important in support staff include the ability to perform a wide variety of tasks, good organizational skills, the ability to grasp the significance and purpose of the work, alertness, accuracy, a sense of responsibility, and good judgment. Since the library is a service department, particular attention should be paid to interpersonal skills. In the absence of the librarian in a small special library, the clerical or library assistant should be competent to keep the routine machinery operating and to handle simple requests for assistance.

The minimum staff recommended for the library is one professional librarian and one clerical employee. In larger libraries, the proportion of two support staff to each professional staff member is often found, but the ratio of professional to support staff varies according to the functions and services performed by the library. As is true at the professional level, the support staff in a small library will need to be extremely versatile. In a larger library, support staff may also specialize, and specific job descriptions require varied skills at various levels.

Occasionally, there may be a need for additional staff to work on special projects, or to cover for regular staff during a leave of absence or vacation, particularly in a library with a small staff. In larger cities there are temporary agencies that specialize in supplying professional, paraprofessional and clerical personnel trained in library and information science. Another option is to contact a local library school and arrange an internship for long-term projects. Information brokers can also be used to supplement research services as the need arises.

The final staffing profile requires detailed planning and operational study of the need for file clerks, secretarial help, technical support staff, reference librarians, and other professional personnel. Varying proportions of types of personnel will have a marked effect on costs, and salaries constitute a major proportion of library expenditures.

LITERATURE CITED

1. Mary Lee Kennedy, "Positioning Strategic Information: Partnering for the Information Advantage," *Special Libraries* 87, no. 2 (Spring 1996): 124.
2. Fay Zipkowitz, "New Directions for Recent Grads," *Library Journal* 120, no. 17 (15 October 1995): 26-33.
3. Ibid.
4. Special Libraries Association, *SLA Biennial Salary Survey 1997* (Washington, DC: Special Libraries Association, 1996).

FURTHER READING

Drotos, Patrick V. "From Online Specialist to Research Manager: Changing With the Times." *Online* 18, no. 1 (January 1994): 54-58.

Giesecke, Joan R. "Mapping a Management Career Using Alternate Routes: An Interview with Sarah Pritchard." *Library Administration & Management* 9, no. 1 (Winter 1995): 6-11.

Hatfield, D. "Partnerships in Information Services: The Contract Library." *Special Libraries* 85, no. 2 (Spring 1994): 77-80.

Marshall, Joanne, Bill Fischer, Lynda Moulton, and Roberta Piccoli. *Competencies for Special Librarians of the 21st Century.* Washington, DC: Special Libraries Association, 1996.

Ojala, Marydee. "Core Competencies for Special Library Managers of the Future." *Special Libraries* 84, no. 4 (Fall 1993): 230-234.

Special Libraries Association. *SLA Biennial Salary Survey 1997.* Washington, DC: Special Libraries Association, 1996.

Sweeney, Del, and Karin Zilla, ed. *Position Descriptions in Special Libraries.* Washington, DC: Special Libraries Association, 1992.

Willner, Richard A. "Education for Library and Information Management Careers in Business and Financial Services." *Library Trends* 42, no. 2 (Fall 1993): 232-248.

CHAPTER

9

What Space and Equipment Are Needed?

Plans for a library's physical facilities should come from an examination of the library's mission, goals, and users, and should reflect a clear understanding of the library's current operations as well as plans for future growth and advancements. This, in turn, should reflect the parent organization's mission, operations, and future plans. A well-designed environment will encourage the use of the library and enhance its effectiveness.

Input from several professions is required in this process. The librarian provides knowledge and experience concerning operations, functional activities, automation requirements, and future needs. An architect or space planner provides solutions for space and structural problems. Management provides the overall policies and direction from the parent organization.

LOCATION

If a library is used by many departments, a convenient central location can stimulate interest in and regular use of the library. If it is used primarily by a particular group, it should be located in that department. While technology enables delivery of some information directly to users' desktops, direct contact between users and the library staff is still necessary for effective delivery of information services.

In a virtual library setting, location may not be as important as in a more traditional setting. Certain situations lend themselves to a virtual library existing simply as librarians working from several well-equipped workstations. In other cases, it means a smaller physical space where the librarian maintains a small core collection of books and periodicals in addition to providing access to internal and external electronic information resources.

Another special consideration in location is the accessibility of the library under the Americans with Disabilities Act of 1991 (ADA). It is important to consider whether any physical barriers exist, either within the library space or outside that space, that would prohibit access to the library or its resources. If those barriers exist, then appropriate accommodations must be made to allow full access to the facility.

AREA USE

Ideally, library space is allocated and organized by functional activities. User space may include a reference area, an area for housing materials and resources, computer workstations, study carrels, group seating, lounge areas, index and abstract tables, display racks, and special equipment areas. The professional and clerical staff work areas include space for ordering, receiving, processing, and organizing materials. The area for administrative functions includes the normal office requirements for conference space, privacy, and operating records. All these functions should be assigned specific locations within the library space. Adequate storage facilities are also necessary.

The nature of the collection has a direct bearing on space requirements. Many libraries need substantial areas to accommodate books, reports, and periodicals on shelving units or stacks. Other libraries house the greater part of their materials in filing cabinets. Special storage equipment may be needed for computer-related data, microfilm, or various audiovisual formats.

The relationships of all library functions should be studied to ensure appropriate and efficient positioning within the library space. The reference desk, catalogs, indexes, reference sources, and current periodical display should be located close to the main library door for convenience and control, while shelving areas, files, cabinet units, and study areas can be positioned farther back. Distinct work areas with partitions may be desired to reduce noise, lessen clutter, minimize disturbance from special equipment, provide privacy, and mask storage and processing activities. An additional library receiving door in the processing area may be desirable to eliminate excessive traffic, particularly from the organization's mail room. It can also double as a fire exit, which may be required by city ordinance.

AREA REQUIREMENTS

A virtual library can be as small as a cubicle with a workstation, while large special libraries may exceed 10,000 square feet (900 square meters). Since there is wide variation in the size of special libraries, it is important to identify all library activities and estimate the space requirements for each. An open rectangular area is most desirable for the library space. Odd spaces are not as efficient but can be designed to accommodate needs.

Forethought in layout, with a minimum of permanent barriers, allows for flexibility and growth and avoids costly moving of heavy shelving and equipment in the future. Library planning should allow for both staff and material expansion over a five-to-ten-year period. During its early years, a new special library's growth rate may be very rapid as a strong, basic resource collection is developed. An established collection can also easily double in size within ten years.

Functional needs plus the number of library staff members should be considered in allocating space. Space allowances for office workers and equipment are generally standardized and well known. However, since the library staff may handle large amounts of materials and use special equipment, extra space is required. Another consideration is that an individual staff member may need more than one work area. For example, a reference librarian may work from a desk in the public reference area but may also need a private work area for support activities.

Space allocation for users depends on their numbers, frequency of visits, time spent in the library, and the type of use made of the facilities. One method of projecting seating requirements suggests one chair for every twenty-five potential users. Another method figures seating for a maximum of ten percent of total users. Various types of seating should be considered. Individual carrels, group tables, lounge chairs, and other arrangements require different amounts of space. Selection of the type of seating depends in part upon whether the library is used for individualized research or as a gathering place for groups to share information.

An advantage of the electronic age is that library staff can work easily with users at many different geographic sites. In such instances, space normally allocated to users is used instead to accommodate a larger library staff.

One factor that is unique to libraries relates to book stack shelving. A standard three-foot-wide library stack section, six shelves high, holds about one hundred volumes with space allowance for growth, though such figures vary according to types and size of special collections or proportion of thicker volumes. Compact shelving or filing systems, although costly, can double capacity. Aisles between book stacks should be no less than three feet wide, to allow for accommodation as set forth by the Americans with Disabilities Act. The weight of the stacks should also be considered, as the building space chosen must be capable of carrying the load.[1]

Minimum Floor Loading Requirements per Square Foot

Type of storage	*Pounds*	*Kilograms*
Stack areas	150	70
Compact shelving	200	90
Filing cabinets	150	68
Microfiche cabinets	200	90

Space for a photocopy machine, microform reader/printer equipment, and audiovisual units should be allocated as necessary. The last two items usually require user seating and easy access to the areas where these materials are stored.

Communication needs should be carefully planned at the outset. Adequate, well-located electrical, telephone, modem jacks, switching facilities, and equipment are essential. If the library is to have a local area network (LAN) or plans one in the future, the cables can be run in the beginning. Locations of computer workstations, printers, fax machines, modems, and other electronic devices should be considered carefully. With technology changing rapidly, it is far better to over plan in this area, adding extra outlets and jacks to allow for future expansion.

If the librarian plans to encourage end user searching on CD-ROM or online products, workstations should be planned not only for library staff but for end users. These workstations should be located close to the reference area so staff on duty can easily help users.

ENVIRONMENT

Generally, the temperature and humidity that are suitable for human comfort are also appropriate for library materials. Rare books and archival papers require lower temperatures. Microform materials need protection from excessive dryness and dust. Adequate air filtration is as important for books as it is for people. Air diffusion may present difficulties in large book stack areas, around movable partition cubicles, or in study rooms.

Computer workstations generate heat and static electricity, which should be taken into account when setting the temperature and humidity. Photocopy, fax, and audiovisual machines also generate heat and noise; it may be necessary to isolate them in a workroom setting or near the library to allow for special environmental controls. Carpeting, acoustical tile, and draperies all absorb sound, while hard surfaces like glass and concrete reflect noise.

LIGHTING

A high level of illumination is desirable and the issues of glare, reflection, absorption, shadowing, and contrast should also be addressed. Ceiling fixtures continuous and perpendicular to the shelving or parallel lighting fixtures attached to each stack unit are recommended and may require special planning in standard office buildings. Reduced or indirect lighting near computer screens is desirable to avoid glare.

WORKSTATIONS

Most staff areas and some user areas in the library are in fact workstations, which combine both furniture and equipment. They may include a combination of standard office furniture and specialized library furnishings. When possible, the library furnishings should compliment those of the rest of the organization in order to further integrate the library into the function of the parent organization. Modular workstations are preferable, as they allow for easy changes in the floor plan.

Each staff workstation has multiple components that may include a personal computer, printer, modem, connection to internal networks, CD-ROM player, and typewriter. User workstations may include a personal computer, modem, printer, microform reader/printer, audiovisual equipment, and CD-ROM player. Because of the multitude of wires, cables, and cords that accompany this equipment, each workstation should have sufficient slots and channels to direct and control them.

Different functions have different needs; for example, a reference workstation may need several pieces of equipment while a library administrator's work center may require only a personal computer. Desks, tables, and countertops should have large work surfaces to allow for processing and use of library materials. Work surfaces should be available on both sides of the equipment to accommodate work flow and multiple users who may be right- or left-handed. Regardless of function, however, each workstation should be designed with ergonomic concerns in mind to prevent repetitive stress injuries.

Workstations may be independent entities, networked within the confines of the library, or connected to a corporate-wide communications system. A LAN to connect library workstations is advantageous when using integrated system software for online catalogs, internal databases, periodical check-in and routing, and acquisitions. At each workstation staff members can access needed parts of the automated system while library users can access an online catalog or database at terminal workstations in the user area. If the library expands to multiple sites, a network system will facilitate communication and link operations.

EQUIPMENT

Library equipment is a combination of standard office furnishings and specialized equipment. Ergonomically appropriate desks and chairs should be provided. File cabinets receive heavier than normal use and must be of good quality; lateral files and legal-size drawers are recommended. Rapid photocopying equipment capable of handling bound volumes should be selected. Requirements for a fax machine should include speed dialing, use of plain cut paper, and a document feed of twenty-five to thirty pages.

Several kinds of specialized library equipment are necessary. Adjustable library shelving of standard dimensions is required to provide efficient and flexible use of space. Commercial manufacturers supply metal book shelving in a variety of colors, together with special attachments such as dividers, sling or slanted shelves, convertible cubicles, and other adaptations. Costs vary according to the size of the installation, discount policies, and similar business arrangements. Costs for double-faced units and add-on sections may be somewhat lower per section. End panels and closed tops are usually additional.

Some special libraries continue to use card index files (card catalogs), especially if the collection is small or unusual. Cards may be used as an initial catalog form while future automation decisions are made and gradually implemented. Library furniture manufacturers supply wooden cabinets in a variety of drawer configurations. A collection of five hundred books requires six to eight drawers of cards, leaving room for expansion. A five-drawer lateral file cabinet containing pamphlets and clippings may require two card catalog drawers of index cards.

Other specialized furniture that may be needed includes carrels, library tables, index tables, dictionary stands, and storage facilities for unusual forms of library materials. Smaller items, such as step stools, a book cart, and a visible file may be necessary.

Providing an appropriate, visible location for the library is the first and most important role management has in space planning. Adequate equipment and furnishings should also be a priority as they make it easy for users to make use of the library and its physical resources. Likewise, should an organization find that a library is more effective for them in a virtual setting, any appropriate allocations for this should be overseen by management. Visiting existing special libraries, reading literature describing the design and equipping of such libraries, communicating with colleagues, and attending business shows or library conferences are good ways to discover new ideas about space use, technology, and equipment that are beneficial to the library and the parent organization.

LITERATURE CITED

1. Richard W. Boss, *Information Technologies and Space Planning for Libraries and Information Centers* (Boston: G.K. Hall Publishers, 1987), 86.

FURTHER READING

Brown, Carol R. *Planning Library Interiors: The Selection of Furnishings for the 21st Century*, 2nd ed. Phoenix: Oryx Press, 1993.

Crispin, Joanne L. ed. *The Americans with Disabilities Act: Its Impact on Libraries and the Library's Response in 'Doable' Steps.* Chicago: American Library Association, 1992.

Foos, Donald D. and Nancy C. Pack, eds. *How Libraries Must Comply with the Americans with Disabilities Act* (ADA). Phoenix: Oryx Press, 1992.

Masyr, Carol, and Robert Freifeld. *Space Planning for Special Libraries.* Washington, DC: Special Libraries Association, 1991.

Matarazzo, James M. *Creative Planning of Special Library Facilities.* New York: Haworth Press, 1988.

CHAPTER

10

How Much Will the Special Library Cost?

"Business pioneers are finding surprising ways to put real dollars on the bottom line as they discover how to measure and manage the ultimate intangible: knowledge."[1]

The special library budget is dependent upon the setting in which the special library is located. Whether the parent organization employs the lump-sum, formula, line, program, performance, or zero-based budgeting process, the budget process should be an integral part of strategic planning.

Libraries can be either cost or profit centers. In cost centers, the budget is built from projected expenditures that are considered overhead. In profit centers, projected expenditures can be offset by projected income. In fact, many libraries use a blend of the two models, recovering some expenditures through rebilling labor and expenses.

Regardless of budget type used by the parent organizations there are some key steps in planning the library's budget process.

1. Tie budget to mission
2. Identify user-base

3. Identify resources at hand and define gaps
4. Use budget tools
5. Estimate expenditures
6. Estimate income
7. Present budget to management
8. Manage budget
9. Plan for next budget cycle

TIE BUDGET TO MISSION

If there is a stated mission of the parent organization and a subordinate mission of the library, the purpose of budget planning is to tie the budget to those mission statements. Every item or expenditure should have a direct link to the mission. What does the parent organization need to know to maintain basic functions and to grow in its respective field or industry? By identifying these critical issues, the library can identify resources necessary to provide information and knowledge necessary to achieve the organization's goals.

IDENTIFY USER BASE

Knowing who the users are helps determine resources required by the library to support them. The size of the primary user group varies by type of organization. A small organization or firm heavily engaged in research may consist almost entirely of library users, while a large manufacturing firm might have a small primary user group. A trade association might include the total membership in the pool of potential users. Some special libraries define the pool of potential users very broadly as anyone who might need information. This view emphasizes the potential reach of the service, but does not usually accurately reflect actual use. By segmenting the potential user population into groups, and applying the results of both published research and information gleaned from an information audit or interviews within the organization, reasonable estimates can be made of the amount and nature of demand likely to be placed on the library.

Defining user groups requires a careful analysis of the pool of potential users. Just as markets for products and services can be segmented by demographic characteristics and by nature of use, so too can the market for information service. Studies of information use indicate that use of the library varies according to such characteristics as type of work (research, marketing, production), level (executive, middle management, technical, clerical), and the purpose for which information is sought (research, planning, keeping up-to-date, fact-checking). The presence or absence of employees with these characteristics has a direct bearing on the number of users and kinds of use the library should expect.

The heaviest use of the library typically comes from a core group of managerial, professional, scientific, and technical personnel involved in research, development, planning, creative, editorial work, or client service. These users demand the most sophisticated information services. Executives and administrative personnel form another significant group of users, usually for competitive intelligence, planning, and development. Operating or production employees and secretarial and clerical staff, on the other hand, usually make less sophisticated use of the library, relying on it chiefly for basic reference and fact-checking purposes.

In some organizations it is necessary to consider outside users as well as those within the organization. For example, a research facility may establish a special library primarily for its staff, but also offer service to outside organizations. Normally services to outside users are limited, so these users should not be counted equally with internal users; on the other hand, some associations actively market library services to members, and potential outside use needs to be weighted more heavily. Even when outside use is not expected to be significant, incidental use and the time required for reciprocal use by other libraries should be expected as a part of normal operations.

IDENTIFY RESOURCES AT HAND AND DEFINE GAPS

What resources are available on an ongoing basis and at what cost? What resources are owned by others, but can be tapped by the library (for instance, an expensive print collection housed in the office of an executive or faculty member)? Perform an information audit or take inventory of the resources already available in the parent organization that the library can tap. Then analyze the gap between what resources are at hand and what is needed to meet the organization's information needs.

USE BUDGET TOOLS

It would be useful to link funding for information service to some quantifiable measure, such as information service as a percentage of the research budget or information service expenditures per user. No such guidelines currently exist. Special libraries differ enormously in functions, services, and budget, even in organizations with similar interests and of comparable size. In addition, the confidential nature of financial information in most organizations prevents the systematic collection of such data. For the organization with a well-established library, it may be quite possible to develop statistics on the library's expenditures as a percentage of the research or other appropriate budget, or per user. Over time this information can serve as a useful indicator of funding levels for information services.

Some tools available for use in developing special library budgets include the following.

- Comparative budget statistics
- Budget ratios
- Staff-user estimates
- Benchmarking
- Engaging a library consultant
- Cost analysis
- Cost and benefits

COMPARATIVE BUDGET STATISTICS

From time to time surveys report expenditures or budget ratios for selected groups of special libraries. Statistics of this nature can be used for comparative purposes and to suggest ranges into which library budgets may fall.

Table 10-1 shows the range of library budgets reported by librarians to the Special Libraries Association.[2] Because these figures exclude salaries, which are a significant portion of the library budget, they represent only partial budgets. When salaries are added, the numbers differ significantly.

BUDGET RATIOS

Another approach to library budget planning is to look at the proportion of the library budget devoted to various categories. These typically

TABLE 10-1
SPECIAL LIBRARY BUDGETS
(excluding salaries), Fiscal 1995

Range	*% of reporting libraries*
Under $25,000	10.2
$25,000-$49,999	7.5
$50,000-$74,999	6.9
$75,000-$99,999	6.8
$100,000-$249,999	17.7
$250,000-$499,999	9.7
$500,000-$749,999	3.6
$750,000-$1,000,000	3.8
Above $1,000,000	10.2
Do not know	23.5

Results of the 1996 Membership Survey, Special Libraries Association.

include salaries, information resources (books, periodicals, online services), equipment, supplies, and so on. Then, if expenditures in at least one category are known, it is possible to extrapolate a total estimated budget using these ratios. The disadvantages to this approach are the differences among special libraries and the fact that only ranges of budget ratios are available. For instance, in a 1988 study of selected libraries in Fortune 500 companies, salary as a percentage of the total budget ranged from 0 to 60%, books from 4 to 20%, journals from 4 to 34%, books and journals combined from 9 to 31%, and online services from 3 to 26%.[3]

STAFF-USER ESTIMATES

Another approach to library budget planning, which perhaps more closely equates library finance to service provided, is estimating the number of users and the desired ratio of library staff to users. Once the user population has been defined, a desirable ratio of library staff members to users can be estimated. Although specific staff-user ratios are not prescribed, various studies and profiles of special libraries, such as *Corporate Library Excellence*, offer staffing examples.[4] The library staff-user ratio will also depend upon the needs and expectations of the parent organization.

BENCHMARKING

Benchmarking, or measuring and comparing performance against other special libraries, is an effective tool for gauging budget requirements. When establishing a library, discussions with similar organizations that already provide library service may be particularly beneficial. By making telephone calls and compiling a few figures, a perception of expenditure norms may develop. In some industries confidentiality may preclude revealing precise budget figures, however, information concerning the various parts that make up a whole budget can probably be obtained.

ENGAGING A LIBRARY CONSULTANT

Engaging a library consultant may be an efficient approach to budget planning when beginning a library. The library consultant can provide guidance in establishing both financial and functional parameters based on the needs of the parent organization. Consultants usually bring years of experience in managing a library as well as the perspective gained in working for a wide variety of libraries in diverse settings.

COST ANALYSIS

Many organizations use cost analysis for purposes of planning, budgeting, and management control. If the organization itself is using cost analysis procedures, the library's system can be set up to parallel what is being done in other departments. A good deal of work on cost analysis has been done within the library and information science field and a body of experience has developed from which the librarian can draw in designing procedures for the collection of data needed for cost decisions.

Basic functions that might be viewed as broad cost categories include the following.

- Direct costs
  - Reference services
    - Ready reference
    - Retrospective searches
  - Program services
    - Current awareness services
- Indirect costs
  - Technical processes
    - Acquisition
    - Organization (cataloging)
  - Administration
    - Maintenance

These may be broken down further in terms of material, personnel, and facility costs, and by the particular unit or project supported. Information on the dollar costs of library functions can be used in planning levels of function, evaluating alternative methods of providing functions and services, estimating the cost of expanding a given function, or starting a new activity. Conversely, if activities must be cut back, cost information aids in determining which functions should be reduced or dropped.

COST AND BENEFITS

Although it is possible to determine the dollar costs of specific library activities and to assess the cost-effectiveness of service alternatives, it is difficult to assign dollar benefits. How does one assign a value to information—to knowing or not knowing? It is possible, in some instances, to put a price tag on a specific piece of information, for example, research costs saved when a literature search identifies the needed information. More often information's contribution is less specific, enhancing thought processes, or providing a basis for more informed decision-making activities that are not quantifiable. Even more amorphous is the concept of the value added by the information professional who transforms a mass of data into useful information. No simple formula can be used to justify information services on an overall basis.

Nevertheless, information professionals are intensely interested in the question of cost benefit and are taking several approaches to research in this area. In a study about library use conducted among almost four hundred randomly selected managers and executives from five major financial institutions in Toronto, the following results were tabulated.[5]

- 70% reported their memory of details or facts was refreshed
- 73% reported it increased their confidence in making a decision
- 42% reported it added a new dimension that they had not thought of before
- 88% reported it provided new knowledge
- 84% reported it led to a better informed decision
- 68% reported it confirmed what they already knew or suspected

The information provided enabled managers and executives to do the following.

- Proceed to the next step on a project or task
- Decide upon a course of action
- Improve the image of the institution
- Improve relations with a client
- Exploit a new business opportunity

The information provided helped managers and executives avoid negative consequences such as the following.

- Loss of their own time
- Loss of another employee's time
- Loss of funds
- Wasting resources such as equipment or supplies
- A poor business decision

Specific examples of cost savings, financial gains, or liabilities avoided can provide evidence of a library's value. Some examples follow.

- A food ingredient supplier discovered that the oil in the plastic packs on one of his products turned green. Engineers at the processing plant asked the technical library for a literature search. The $11 online search yielded the answer and saved an estimated two hundred hours of laboratory work.[6]

- Another company learned from the librarian's routine patent search that a package being developed might infringe on another newly patented package and thus avoided approximately $20 million in possible damages and legal fees.[7]

Examples like these provide dramatic evidence of the value of library services but they only highlight specific instances of service rather than illuminating the entire picture.

Another way of looking at the value of library services is based on time and money saved when library staff, rather than the users, locate the information, thus freeing the users time to pursue activities in which they are more expert. This method also demonstrates the efficiency of the information professional in literature searching and reference service, two basic and important library activities.

- A company library conducted a survey concerning the hours saved on literature searches. It was found that "for every hour the library spent literature searching, we saved the engineering staff 8.86 hours of effort."[8]

- This library also investigated the time saved on short reference questions and requests to identify a publication. Here an average savings of 5.42 hours per request was reported. The average time spent by the library was twelve minutes per request.[9]

- A study of users conducting searches in small high tech businesses found that the average cost of a search was nearly $4,000, of which $3,715 was spent in user time, preparing and negotiating the search and examining the results, while the same search, conducted by information specialists, cost only $300.[10]

The benefits of current awareness services are particularly difficult to quantify because much of the benefit of keeping up with developments in a field is nonspecific. One series of research studies on information use among companies and government agencies found that reading books, journals, and technical reports resulted in a ten to one return on investment. These results are based on the average return from three perspectives, willingness to pay for information provided by the library, the cost of alternative sources for the information, and estimates of what benefits would be lost if the library did not exist.[11] Another study of the value of the benefits of disseminating literature to technical research personnel found that the ratio of net benefits to expenditures was eleven to one.[12]

A watershed 1993 analysis based on twenty-seven independent studies of sixteen companies, seven governmental agencies, and four national surveys of professionals yielding more than ten thousand statistical survey responses, quantified the contribution that libraries make to their organizations. The authors of the study summarize these data as follows, "Including both services that lead to use of documents and those that do not include materials, we find that such return-on-investment is 2.9 to 1."[13]

These examples show that the benefits of library service can be very great. They also illustrate the difficulties of measuring services and benefits and how complex such studies can be. Such intangibles as information's impact on the general knowledge of the organization's personnel, improved decision making, improved productivity, and greater efficiency, all of which lead to more effective management and better profitability, are not easily translated into economic terms.

Knowledge is valuable to any organization. Associating a cost with this value is difficult, however, one company is attempting to do just that. Sweden's Skandia AB is including the value of information in its Annual Report.

ESTIMATE EXPENDITURES

Organizational policies for setting budget categories differ. Some organizations include salaries and benefits in unit budgets, others do not. Overhead charges such as space, utilities, and communications may not be included. In preparing the budget for an individual special library, such variations must be taken into account. However, since the purpose of this section is to provide guidelines for budget planning, the basic categories of salaries, publications, online computer services, internal computer services, outside services, and other budget items such as equipment, supplies, and travel are described.

SALARIES

Salaries for staff are one of the larger expenditure categories in the special library. The size and composition of the staff are determined by a number of factors including the size of the user base, demand for information services, and the subject matter or discipline searched. Staffing issues are discussed in detail in Chapter 8.

INFORMATION RESOURCES

Information resources include online databases, CD-ROMs, data feeds, news at desktops, books, periodicals, indexes, documents, reports, software, systems, and services, and represent the largest or second largest expenditure (after salaries) in most special libraries. Here it is necessary to consider whether journals are more numerous and important than books, whether back files are needed, whether they should be in their original form, microform, or CD-ROM, and to what extent access to online databases affects the need for print copies of indexes and journals. If publications in several subject fields are needed and thorough coverage is necessary, the library will acquire more information resources than if only one field is covered. Also, costs of information resources vary considerably by subject area as Table 10-2 illustrates.[14]

TABLE 10-2
PERIODICAL TITLE COST DIFFERENCES BY SUBJECT, 1996

Subject	*Average cost*	*% change 1992–96*
Business and economics	$280.86	67.10
Engineering	$715.78	61.35
Health sciences	$486.35	54.60
Law	$113.02	40.05
Music	$62.582	5.03
Physics	$1,354.80	58.06

Lee Ketcham and Kathleen Born, "36th Annual Report Periodical Price Survey 1996: Projecting the Electronic Revolution While Budgeting for the Status Quo," *Library Journal* 121, no. 7 (15 April 1996): 46.

External Online Databases. Almost all special libraries use external online databases to search for historical and current information on either an ongoing or ad hoc basis. Generally, libraries contract with several different online services or vendors who offer access to multiple databases.

There may be an initial sign-up fee, minimum-use charges, and a combination of connect time fees, search fees, and output-based fees (by character, field, lines, format, page, story, document, or report). Experienced searchers can minimize database searching costs not only by determining which services and databases to use, but by structuring searches and online time to achieve the most effective results at the least cost.

Predicting level of use and searching costs is difficult for the special library, whether existing or new. User demand is hard to predict. For this reason, many information providers offer fixed price contracts based on past usage and reevaluate the contracts at specific intervals (every six months or year). Fixed-price contracts do make budgeting these costs easier. Database expenditures reported in some surveys often do not reflect the common practice of passing along search charges to users, resulting in under reporting of database expenditures.

CD-ROM Databases. Directories, company reports, compilations of Securities and Exchange Commission filings, census data, research reports, reference books, and periodical indexes with abstracts or full text documents are all found in CD-ROM format. Libraries purchase CD-ROM products on a fixed-price subscription basis, which makes budget planning easier. Prices vary greatly by product ranging from under $100 to over $100,000 per year. In addition to the basic price, costs may depend on the number of updates issued (monthly, quarterly, annually), inclusion of data from previous years, software complexity, and joint purchase of print copy. A local area network (LAN) license usually costs more than a single PC license, and the cost increases with the number of users.

Periodicals. Due to the demand for current information, the increasing number of journals published, and the ability to search the journal via online databases, periodicals and newsletters may be the centerpiece of a library's current physical collection. Special library periodical collections vary. One survey showed a range from 180 to 5,000 titles.[15] Some libraries do not subscribe to or collect many hard copies of periodicals, opting to use electronic sources and document delivery services to order articles as needed. Subscriptions to specialized newsletters may be double or triple the cost of standard periodical subscriptions. Some publishers offer discounts on multiple copies of their publications. In some fields, controlled circulation trade journals are sent to organizations free of charge. Also, in some fields, electronic journals available on the Internet are also changing periodical subscription budgets and procedures.

Reference. These are sources such as periodical indexes, abstract services, statistical services, legal reports for commercial, patent, or labor law, and similar publications. In many fields such services are an important part of the collection. Costs vary considerably; for instance some statistical publications from government entities are very inexpensive or free, while some extensive statistical services compiled by private firms cost thousands of dollars. As with other information resources, costs also vary from one field or subject to another.

Specialized Materials. Many special libraries acquire more reports, documents, and pamphlets than they do books. Some maintain collections of more than 500,000 technical reports. Some materials are free or inexpensive while others can cost several thousand dollars. Therefore, it is difficult to generalize costs. Technical reports, patents, standards, and census data are often available in microform or via computer formats, which are usually less expensive and available earlier than their hard copy counterparts.

Books. The number of books purchased per year may range from fewer than 100 to as many as 5,000. Data for thirty-three libraries shows that five libraries acquired more than 2,000 books annually, averaging 4,800 items, five libraries acquired between 1,000 and 2,000 books annually with an average of 1,200, and twenty-three libraries acquired fewer than 1,000 books annually, averaging 448 purchases per year.[16] Again, prices vary considerably depending on subject area and the country in which they are published. A basic business reference collection of 200 titles was estimated to cost $38,000 in 1993.[17]

SOFTWARE

Software requirements include both general office and specialized library applications. Like other departments or functions, libraries use a wide variety of general office software including word processing, telecommunications, database management, groupware, Internet browsers, spreadsheets, presentation, and project management. Specialized library applications include online catalogs, automated interlibrary loan systems, shared cataloging systems, and automated indexing systems. Integrated library systems that handle periodical control, routing, acquisitions, cataloging, and circulations can also be purchased. Software is usually purchased gradually as library functions are automated, but a new library may have significant startup costs to meet basic needs. The budget should also include the cost of maintenance contracts and periodic software upgrades.

Some automated library operations may be located on in-house computer equipment shared with other departments. Special internal software programs or systems may be written or adapted by in-house personnel to accommodate library functions. The library may be charged for time and space on this equipment or for maintenance of these in-house localized or networked automated systems.

OUTSIDE SERVICES

Funds may be needed to pay translators or to engage systems, programming, or consulting assistance. Commercial information broker services or temporary personnel may be required for special research projects outside the scope of library resources or occasionally to augment library personnel. Costs for information broker services can range from $500 to $1,500 or more per project. These rates may be reduced by negotiating an annual fee or retainer if there is a need for regular support. Libraries will occasionally require the services of temporary agencies, some of which specialize in staffing libraries, for short or long term projects and vacations. The budget should include projected costs for hourly clerical or professional temporary staff.

DOCUMENT DELIVERY

Document delivery involves obtaining material not in the library through either interlibrary loan or commercial services. While some libraries provide library-to-library transactions free or at minimal cost, commercial services that guarantee timeliness and quality are also widely available. Transaction charges may depend on volume of use. Per article costs range from $10 to $25. Rush, fax, and special handling transactions usually cost more. Libraries can also establish deposit accounts to speed delivery and simplify payment. Trade association libraries may offer their members discounts. Since materials acquired for a fee supplement the library's own collection, funds allocated to document delivery may also be found in the budget under publications rather than outside services.

OTHER BUDGET ITEMS

The remainder of the budget is similar to other departmental budgets in the organization. Overhead costs such as insurance, social security, and benefit plan deductions are charged the same as the rest of the organization. Other categories customarily included are discussed below.

Equipment. This category may vary considerably from year to year. Some examples include computer hardware, furnishings, microform readers and storage cabinets, shelving, ladders, stools, and equipment rental or repair. Provisions should be made for gradually adding and replacing items as services and the size of the collection grow. In years when the library's space expands or it moves to new quarters, larger expenditures for new equipment should be planned as part of expansion costs.

Supplies. This includes standard office supplies and such special items as catalog cards and book pockets. Some specially printed forms may be needed for circulation records, order records, indexing work sheets, periodical record cards, or form memos of various kinds.

Professional Development and Travel. As is the case for professional and managerial personnel in other departments, funds are usually provided for professional library staff members to attend meetings and conferences. Some organizations establish special funds for visits to other libraries or information centers when a new library is planned, to arrange for special services, or when expansion into new fields requires the library staff to become acquainted quickly with the resources in libraries working in those fields. Funds for sending staff members to various training programs, institutes, and short courses may also be included. These funds are very important to include since developments in information management are occurring rapidly, and such courses are an effective way of keeping up with the changes. Funds for these activities might also be allocated under staff development or tuition reimbursement.

Miscellaneous Expenses. Other expenses might include memberships, printing and graphics for marketing brochures, postage, and telephone costs. A petty cash fund or credit card is also desirable since it is often necessary to obtain a book or publication quickly, send messengers, or reimburse another library for photocopies.

ESTIMATE INCOME

Expenditures can be offset in whole or in part by charging for library services. In many cases, library service charges are simply a means of identifying and allocating costs. The information service costs recorded by the library can be assigned on a regular pay-as-you-go basis to the specific departments, projects, clients, or other identifiable units that incur them. In a variation on this approach, the library's budget may be based on allocations or assessments from user departments, based on either previous or anticipated use.

Another method applied, particularly in professional service firms, is to actually bill the client for library services along with other organizational services performed. This method creates additional income for the organization.

A few libraries sell some products or services—online databases, research services, publications—directly to outside users. Such products or services can be priced on a for-profit basis. This, too, creates income for the organization. Libraries can recover some costs this way, but few are able to become self-supporting or even recover a major portion of their costs.

Cost recovery offers a number of distinct advantages. By charging users for the services they receive, the library demonstrates in concrete terms its contributions to the organization. Users become more aware that the service has value. Cost recovery for library services also reduces the otherwise unallocated overhead of the organization and improves identification of the costs of doing business.

There are also, however, strong arguments against charging for services. One argument is that putting a price tag on the use of the library may actually inhibit the use of information as potential library users try to economize by doing without needed information. This conflicts directly with the organization's interest in encouraging use of the library's information services to further corporate goals. A second argument against charging for services is that the inevitable pressure felt by the library staff to maximize billable time has a negative effect on the nonbillable administrative and support functions that are necessary to the efficient functioning of the library as a whole. To counter this pressure, some libraries differentiate between billable and nonbillable positions and activities. Necessary administrative and support positions and activities continue as overhead to ensure an adequate level of support for basic operations. Direct service time and activities, on the other hand, may be classified as billable, which can work to the library's advantage if the additional income generated can be used to add additional billable staff positions. It is also possible to protect support functions by including library overhead in calculating charges.

In any consideration of charging back or billing, the organizational culture should be taken into account. If no other service departments charge back, there may be resistance. If others charge, then library charge backs are more likely to be accepted. The library should follow the parent organization's policies and practices in cost recovery. Yet, even in cases where the library is carried as overhead, it is wise to maintain records of costs for planning the budget as well as for potential institution of cost recovery in the future.

PRESENT BUDGET TO MANAGEMENT

The librarian presents the budget to management in the style in which other departments present theirs, using computerized projected displays, slide presentations, overheads, spreadsheets, reports, executive summaries, or a combination of the above.

MANAGE BUDGET

It is advisable to keep close tabs on the expenditures as the budget year progresses. Print outs from the accounting department help the librarian keep abreast of the current status of expenditures and income, if any. As the year progresses, adjustments may become necessary. It is helpful if some flexibility exists by which resources can be reallocated should some organizational or user priorities change.

PLAN FOR NEXT BUDGET CYCLE

Even as the current budget is in process, next year's budget can be in its infancy. As longer term needs are identified, the resources necessary become the basis of future budget plans. Inflation attacks libraries, too (see Table 10-2). Within a year the figures presented here will be obsolete. Organizations that merely want to maintain current levels of service must increase the library budget to match the level of inflation in information services. Librarians can apply many cost containment measures, but an annual inflation rate of seven or eight percent over a period of years must be offset by budget increases in order to maintain effective information services.[18] Checking the Consumer Price Index, publishing industry references, and library journals for inflation rates, as well as double checking with internal procedures and recommendations, enables the librarian to bring the library budget in line with internal and external cost environments.

The library's budgeting process is linked to the mission of the parent organization. An understanding of the direction and needs of the user base drives the decisions on how the library allocates resources that help the organization create, organize, disseminate, protect, and use its knowledge.

LITERATURE CITED

1. Thomas A. Stewart, "Your Company's Most Valuable Asset: Intellectual Capital," *Fortune* (3 October 1994): 68.
2. Results of the 1996 Membership Survey, Special Libraries Association.
3. Tobi A. Brimsek, compiler, *From the Top: Profiles of U.S. and Canadian Corporate Libraries and Information Centers* (Washington, DC: Special Libraries Association, 1989).
4. James M. Matarazzo, *Corporate Library Excellence* (Washington, DC: Special Libraries Association, 1990).
5. Joanne G. Marshall, Ph.D., *The Impact of the Special Library on Corporate Decision-Making,* (Washington, DC: Special Libraries Association, 1993), 70.
6. James B. Tchobanoff, "The Impact Approach: Value as Measured by the Benefit of the Information Professional to the Parent Organization" in *Final Report of the President's Task Force of the Value of the Information Professional* (Washington, DC: Special Libraries Association, 1987), 46.
7. Ibid., 45.

8. Joseph Kramer "How to Survive in Industry, Cost Justifying Services," *Special Libraries* 62, no. 11 (1971): 487-89.
9. Ibid.
10. Miriam A. Drake, "Value of the Information Professional Cost/Benefit Analysis," in *Final Report of the President's Task Force on the Value of the Information Professional* (Washington, DC: Special Libraries Association, 1987), 19.
11. Ibid.
12. Ben H. Weil, "Benefits from Research Use of the Published Literature at the Exxon Research Center." in *Special Librarianship: A New Reader*, ed. Eugene B. Jackson (Metuchen, NJ: Scarecrow Press, 1980), 586-594.
13. Jose-Marie Griffiths and Donald W. King, *Special Libraries: Increasing the Information Edge* (Washington DC: Special Libraries Association, 1993), 1, 187-188.
14. Lee Ketcham and Kathleen Born, "36th Annual Report Periodical Price Survey 1996: Projecting the Electronic Revolution While Budgeting for the Status Quo," *Library Journal* 121, no. 7 (15 April 1996): 46.
15. Mount, Ellis, *Special Libraries and Information Centers: An Introductory Text*, 3rd ed. (Washington DC: Special Libraries Association, 1995).
16. Brimsek, *From the Top*.
17. Bernard S. Schlessinger, ed. and Rashelle S. Karp, associate ed., *The Basic Business Library Core Resources*, (Phoenix: Oryx Press, 1995), vii.
18. Kathryn Hammell Carpenter and Adrian W. Alexander, "U.S. Periodical Price Index for 1996," *American Libraries* 27, no. 5 (May 1996): 99.

FURTHER READING

Danilenko, Gene. "Activity Based Costing for Services: The Corporate Information Center." *Special Libraries* 85, no. 1 (Winter 1994): 24-29.

Ferguson, Elizabeth, and Emily R. Mobley. *Special Libraries at Work*. Hamden, CT: Library Professional Publications, 1984, 100-104.

Finney, Robert G. "Budgeting: From Pain to Power." *Management Review* 82, no. 9 (September 1993): 27-31.

____. "Budgeting: Planning for the Unknown." *Management Review* 82, no. 10 (October 1993): 20-23.

Grisold, R. E. "How to Link Strategic Planning With Budgeting." CMA —*The Management Accounting Magazine* 69, no. 6 (July-August 1995): 21.

McClenahen, John S. "Generally Accepted Practice? The Pluses—and Minuses—of Activity-Based Budgeting." *Industry Week* 244, no. 20 (6 November 1995): 13-14.

Mount, Ellis. *Special Libraries and Information Centers: An Introductory Text,* 3rd ed. Washington, DC: Special Libraries Association, 1995, 47-60.

Rounds, Richard S. *Basic Budgeting Practices for Librarians*, 2nd ed. Chicago: American Library Association, 1994.

Schmidt, Jeffrey A. "Is It Time to Replace Traditional Budgeting?" *Journal of Accountancy* 174, no. 4 (October 1992): 103-107.

Skandia AB. Annual Report 1995.

Stewart, Thomas. "Your Company's Most Valuable Asset: Intellectual Capital." *Fortune* 130, no. 7 (3 October 1994): 68-70.

Stewart, Thomas, and Shawn Tully. "Why Budgets Are Bad for Business." *Fortune* 121, no. 13 (4 June 1990): 179-190.

Warner, Alice Sizer. "Library Budget Primer." *Wilson Library Bulletin* (May 1993): 44-46.

Warner, Alize Sizer. *Owning Your Numbers: An Introduction to Budgeting for Special Libraries.* Washington, DC: Special Libraries Association, 1992.

CHAPTER

11

Alternative Roles for Information Professionals

"Librarians themselves are stepping out of the role of information gopher and into that of organizer, value assessor and teacher . . . designers, facilitators and analyzers of information."[1]

In the last several years, prominent management consultants and academics such as Peter Drucker and Tom Peters have noted the growing importance of information as a competitive weapon, and have emphasized the need to manage it well. At the same time other business writers lament the lack of personnel trained to effectively manage information. Taking special librarians out of the library, removing them from the traditional setting and stereotypical role, provides the organization with information professionals with the skills, experience, and motivation to perform a broad variety of information management tasks.

Special librarians are the first to acknowledge the dramatic changes taking place in information management. They realize that the whole arena of information retrieval and distribution is changing, and that they need to change with it. Professional association programs, continuing education classes, conferences, and chapter meetings frequently focus on skill enhancement and the changing functions involved in information management. Librarians are excited about the changes taking place, aware of the need to change the way they do their jobs, and willing to explore new roles and ways to put their skills to work for the benefit of their employers.

OPPORTUNITIES FOR CHANGE

There are a number of situations in which organizations can benefit from considering alternative roles for information professionals. For instance, an organization recognizing the need to better manage information may, after careful consideration, decide that it cannot commit the resources to establish a library. It may be possible for such an organization to take a smaller step toward information management—it isn't necessary to undertake the entire traditional library operation with a formal facility to reap the benefits of having an information professional on staff. Much can be done by such a person placed within any department with the need to manage information.

An organization with a decentralized structure or culture that does not lend itself to a central library facility may benefit from an information professional in a central administrative role to manage, coordinate, or act as liaison for scattered research activities undertaken in various departments. Or, an organization with a library facility may be faced with the need to manage information beyond the traditional library setting. In this situation the special librarian on staff can take on an expanded role; this would be particularly advantageous if the librarian has hit a career plateau and is looking for a renewed challenge and responsibilities within the organization. With or without traditional libraries, librarians promote effective information sharing methods—a growing area of management concern.

The most difficult situation requiring a nontraditional approach is when an organization must cut staff. Information management skills are highly transferable, and special librarians are accustomed to shifting the nature of their activities to address changes in their organizations, as well as in the changing information environment. If handled correctly, repositioning information professionals is a win-win situation. Librarians have an opportunity to expand their experience, and managers find creative ways to deal with cutbacks or hiring freezes without losing seasoned employees.

Special librarians who have managed an operation also have skills above and beyond their expertise as an information professional. Special librarians run what are essentially small businesses within organizations, using a variety of management skills that have applications in many work situations. Many have a very entrepreneurial attitude and encourage creative solutions to information problems, an approach that can benefit an organization in or out of a library.

SKILLS

The skills of special librarians are summarized below by general roles in order to consider them in a broader context or "outside of the box." These skills can be used in a variety of positions within an organization. Librarians bring key characteristics to any task: curiosity and desire for continuous learning, persistence in pursuit of an answer, and the desire to provide a useful service. Their broad business experience and knowledge of the organization's structure and function are also an asset. The Special Libraries Association has also outlined the competencies of today's information professionals; these can be found in Appendix E.

INFORMATION CONSULTING

Librarians know how a group or organization uses information. They monitor overall information needs and help individuals determine what information they need to do their jobs. They know what resources fill particular needs, where to find them, how to get them, and how to evaluate them.

INFORMATION MANAGEMENT

Librarians develop processes for handling large quantities of information in paper, microform or computerized formats. They know how to organize information in a manner that is easily navigated by end users.

DATABASE DEVELOPMENT

Librarians know information technology, database construction and search software. They know how to define the need to be addressed and determine appropriate content. They know how to index and abstract data for easy retrieval. They are familiar with the way end users pose queries.

END USER TRAINING

Librarians provide instruction and support for a variety of computer databases, news delivery services, and groupware programs. They have experience searching electronic databases, are experts at search techniques, and are familiar with potential pitfalls of online searching. Their experience handling reference questions makes them familiar with end user needs and the way end users are likely to approach questions.

RESEARCH AND ANALYSIS

Librarians are skilled at defining information needs and performing research, have a network of experts and other contacts to draw on, and have the communication skills to present the results in a variety of formats.

WRITING, PUBLISHING AND EDITING

Librarians summarize research in reports, write abstracts, index, compile bibliographies or directories, edit newsletters, develop marketing materials, and write user manuals.

SERVICE MANAGEMENT

Librarians know the issues involved in providing a service. They know how to define the group to be addressed and determine its needs. They prepare budgets, supervise and train staff, and determine what resources are necessary to deliver the service in question.

PLANNING AND DECISION MAKING

Librarians have strong problem solving skills. They use surveys and are familiar with survey design, sampling, and statistical techniques. They also perform needs assessments. In both cases they evaluate and present results.

USING INFORMATION SKILLS OUTSIDE OF THE LIBRARY

As organizations move away from the warehouse model of the library, managers realize that utilization and management of information does not take place only in the library. Librarians fill the roles discussed below as part of established library operations, as part of a strategy using a virtual library or knowledge management facilities, or on their own, within particular departments or serving the organization as a whole.

KNOWLEDGE MANAGEMENT

There is an increased focus on internal information produced by the employees of an organization, and the need to manage it well. The result is usually knowledgebases and intranets. There are many roles information professionals can play in this arena. A fundamental tenet of the library profession is to promote the sharing of information.

Librarians have led the development of knowledge management at a number of organizations. Librarians have experience identifying internal deposits of information through the information audit process. They know how to index, abstract, and organize information in a manner promoting easy retrieval by users. On the technical side, librarians are familiar with the groupware used for these programs, and have experience with information retrieval from electronic databases of all kinds. They have used a myriad of search engines, from simple point and click graphical interfaces, to complex command-driven systems, and are intimately acquainted with the potential difficulties of online searching. Librarians are also familiar with the way users pose queries, and how they are likely to approach a question.

> Librarians at a home-building materials manufacturing company were instrumental in the design and implementation of an online knowledge resource center, which integrated in-house databases and online content providers into one facility. They organized the resources so that users could start with broad topics and drill down to more specific information, with decisions based on topical clues, eliminating the need for them to try to guess which source might be the best to answer a question.[2]

In the function of user support, librarians have experience teaching users how to use electronic databases on CD-ROM, online systems, and the Internet. They are proactive in marketing information products, promoting their use, and helping users adapt to new information tools. Librarians can help employees formulate contributions to a knowledge management system, making suggestions as to what others in the organization might be looking for or find valuable. They also develop information resources themselves, extracted from pertinent external sources, integrating internal and external information in a single facility.

> A consulting firm developed a knowledge management system and set up a hotline support service staffed by two research analysts. If the research analysts cannot help users find what they need in the knowledgebase, the request is passed on to two information specialists or librarians on call as custom researchers. The research results, unless they are proprietary, are added to the knowledgebase. Custom research requests are tracked and calls to the hotline are logged; both are reviewed periodically to determine what areas of content need to be developed.[3]

COMPETITIVE INTELLIGENCE

This is a focused information retrieval and dissemination role in which the researcher gathers information on an organization's competitors and marketplace, and speeds delivery of that information to staff in key development, marketing, and decision-making positions. Librarians working within an organization generally know who needs what, where to get it, how to distill it to the most useful form, and what delivery method will get it to users in a quick and convenient manner. They also have experience working with current awareness services used to disseminate published information directly to interested parties. Librarians develop a network of experts in the field, and establish contacts for obtaining unpublished information. It is becoming more common to find people who are members of both the Special Libraries Association (SLA) and the Society of Competitive Intelligence Professionals (SCIP).

> The librarian is part of a team doing competitive intelligence research at a large regional financial institution. She set up online clipping services and arranged for training from database vendors so users could do their own searching. She helps them with more complex searches or does the research for them. She also located a nearby association library in their field and arranged for them to have access to resources and experts there. Members of this team network extensively, and attend SLA and SCIP conferences.[4]
>
> The above example is not unique. A competing national financial institution has a similar arrangement with the information professionals in its library.[5]

TRAINING

One of the information management changes taking place is a move toward direct access to information resources by end users using a personal computer. Networked CD-ROMs, news delivery systems such as NewsWatch, NewsEDGE, and Paracel, databases accessible through groupware such as Lotus Notes, and the Internet all fall into this category. The introduction of these products is exciting, and they are easier to use than online systems of the past, but they are not yet intuitive for most people. Organizations that use these tools find that there are substantial training and support issues involved. Users need ongoing support and training above and beyond what is offered by vendors. In many cases information professionals are taking on the training role.

A significant user training issue for all desktop tools is teaching users how to perform searches effectively. This would be an easier task if there was standard search software used by all database producers or vendors, but this is not the case. While simple searches, such as a well-known company name, might be successful, more specific searches are often necessary, are more exacting to construct, and differ from one search engine to another. This type of information access is attractive to many upper-level managers who often have limited experience with personal computers. Anecdotal evidence indicates that they need ongoing support at a moment's notice, as they use these systems to follow breaking news events.

Another training issue is helping users decide where to go for what information, and which source is the best for a particular need. This is a particularly hot issue with the Internet. The hype accompanying the World Wide Web in particular, has led users to expect to get any information imaginable, free, at the click of a button. In truth the information available on the Internet is much less comprehensive. Librarians have taken on the job of teaching users how to use the Internet, educating them about what kind of information they can expect to get from resources available there, and what alternative resources are available when the using the Internet is not appropriate. While others focus on the technical aspects, librarians focus on the content. They develop guides, some in the form of web pages, to help users find useful information in what is often an overwhelming maze.[6]

> Librarians at a physics laboratory developed a training course to help research and development staff productively use Internet resources. Basic goals were to teach users to configure

> and use browser software, to understand how the Internet and its components work, and to identify and use relevant information resources. They also developed a World Wide Web site with links to resources pertinent to the work done at the lab, as well as a homepage offering technical and business-related information.[7]

> A former university librarian at Boston College now teaches at BC's Carroll School of Management and consults with companies on how they can make use of the Internet. She has recently written a book, *The Internet Strategy Handbook,* which contains case studies detailing what different companies have done.[8]

Resources available through all of the above technologies are constantly changing, making it desirable to have someone focused on helping users find the most reliable and complete information quickly and at a reasonable cost, in terms of both time and money. The alternative is to have users spending copious amounts of time trying to find something useful and current, with the risk that the information they do find is unreliable.

WEB SITE DEVELOPMENT OR WEBMASTER

The appeal of the Internet, and the World Wide Web in particular, is easy access to information. As noted, however, above, finding useful information is not always easy. Another way librarians can make the Internet more useful is to organize the information that is made available there. Even on the Web, information has to be organized in a logical manner if users are to find it with a minimum of time and effort. Who better to do this than the people who have been doing it for years? Organizational concepts and finding tools are as applicable to the Web as they are to other information resources. A number of organizations are realizing that there is a role for librarians to play in the development of Web resources.

> Librarians at a technology company were asked to develop a place where employees could put reports they wanted to share with others at the company. They developed an intranet and maintain the corporate web site, handling company-wide information. Specific departmental information is represented by links to departmental sites, which are maintained by their respective departments.[9]

Another issue in using the Internet and intranets is ensuring that resources used are productive and useful. As one information systems manager put it, "In the era of the Web, everyone has become a writer. But now we need some editors."[10] A key role for librarians is another one they've performed before—identifying user needs and matching them to appropriate resources. Librarians filter out the less useful resources and bring the most useful resources to users' attention by participating in the development of the organization's web pages, ensuring that useful links are easy to find and kept up-to-date. They can also advise on other information issues, such as copyright infringement.

> A global chemical company has a cross-functional team of three people advising the staff who manage the content of the company's web site. The library manager is a member of this team, giving advice on content organization, security issues regarding proprietary research and development information, and copyright issues.[11]

> Another technology company formed an internal service group to act as consultants for groups putting material on the company intranet, educating them about "common look and feel and writing for online consumption." This service group, which works in partnership with information systems staff, is lead by a librarian who explains their relationship, "They do the technology; we do the information management."[12]

OTHER ROLES TO CONSIDER

TEAM MEMBER

An information professional can be an important member of any team in which information must be gathered, analyzed, and presented either to others in the organization or to outside clients. As a researcher, information consultant, trainer, and writer or presenter, the information professional can articulate capabilities of a variety of resources to meet the team's information needs and help other team members use them effectively.

> A consulting firm has librarians assigned to case teams working on client projects, helping team members use desktop tools effectively, performing the more sophisticated research for them as needed, and providing customized service according to the needs of the project.[13]

DOCUMENT OR RECORDS MANAGEMENT

Document or records management involves many of the same skills and tools as other information management roles previously discussed. Whether information is on paper, microform, or in computerized format, the logical organization of the information within, and user access to it, are the fundamental tasks at hand.

> The corporate information systems department of a technology firm developed an online document management system, with repositories for everything from competitive intelligence to the company's telephone directory to policy manuals. Librarians indexed and organized the material. They also worked with publishers to make sure journal articles included were electronic text from publishers and not merely scanned-in versions, making full text searches possible with a variety of search engines.[14]

> A librarian is a manager in the Records and Information Management Department of an HMO. She manages the people who handle the HMO's forms and records, and is part of a team implementing an imaging project to optically scan records currently on paper and microfiche and store them on laser disc.[15]

MARKET RESEARCH

Business librarians often do market research in the course of their reference work, as marketing departments are usually heavy library users. Librarians are able to familiarize themselves with a new topic or client quickly, and their well-developed communication skills enable them to summarize and present information in a variety of formats.

> Law firms are now including librarians on teams preparing to market the firm's services to particular corporate clients. They compile a package of information on the company including financial information, payment and credit history, officer and director biographies, press coverage, federal and state filings, information on pending suits, and corporate transactions, as well as industry background and competition.[16]

PUBLIC RELATIONS

Librarianship and public relations both require creativity, problem solving skills, and the ability to respond quickly in a critical situation.

Librarians have the ability to conduct a reference interview to define an information need, are familiar with resources held throughout the organization, and know the organization and its functions, making them good candidates for the job. Government agencies often take advantage of these skills by making library managers Freedom of Information Act contacts for their agencies.

> A former librarian is managing partner of a public relations firm. She recognizes several skills and characteristics typical of librarians as applicable to public relations: the ability to track down leads, sense trends, write, assess problems, and develop a strategy to solve them. Again the fundamental skills are the ability to gather, organize, and present information.[17]

NEWSLETTER EDITOR

The same fundamental skills of gathering, organizing, and presenting information, often by a particular deadline, apply to writing. Librarians also have experience interviewing people, and are persistent in pursuit of hard-to-find information. Librarians know their audience and what information would be of interest to them. Their experience using a broad variety of information resources makes them knowledgeable about how to present different types of information successfully.

> An information professional, holding a master of science degree in library science, is an editorial researcher for *Internet World* magazine. She writes a monthly column, "Cyberlibrarian," highlighting web sites on a different topic each month.

INFORMATION VENDOR RELATIONSHIP MANAGER OR PURCHASING AGENT

The trend to provide electronic delivery of information to the desktop was mentioned earlier in regard to knowledge management and training. Another issue raised by this approach is the need to manage the relationship with the vendor. Librarians advise on product and vendor selection, ensuring that products chosen meet user needs, and translate those user needs for the vendor. The relationship manager arranges for user training, handles contracts, payments to the vendor, and internal cost distribution as appropriate. Librarians know, and have relationships with, the vendors in this arena. They are familiar with competing vendors, their reputations, product content, delivery options, user interfaces, and the varied pricing strategies they offer. Putting an experienced librarian in this role ensures selection of appropriate products at an appropriate cost.

The roles discussed here represent only a few of the different ways an organization can utilize the skills of librarians or information professionals. Whether an organization is looking for ways to manage information without a formal library, in addition to a library, with a virtual library, or after a library has been downsized, there are many ways in which information professionals can have a significant impact.

THINK 'INFORMATION MANAGEMENT' RATHER THAN 'LIBRARY'

In an article on the future of knowledge management, Tom Davenport, a colleague of Drucker and Peters, and a leading proponent of the effective use of information, states the following.

> In the rosy future I envision, categorization and organization of knowledge will be a core competence for every firm. This will require strategic thinking about what knowledge is important; development of a knowledge vocabulary (and a thesaurus to accommodate near misses); prolific creation of indices, search tools and navigation aids; and constant refinement and pruning of knowledge categories. Knowledge editors will have to combine sources and add context to transform information into knowledge.[18]

Categorization and organization, thesauri of knowledge vocabulary, indices, search tools, and navigation aids are all tools of the information profession developed by librarians. Librarians continue to participate in translating them for use in new media, and continue to reexamine how they can be applied to better manage information. Davenport continues, "In the future, the scarce commodity in knowledge management will be attention. No one firm does all these things well today, but the skills to do them are most commonly found among librarians and print journalists."[19]

Davenport recognizes that librarians have the skills needed for effective information management. The examples presented in this chapter show that he is not alone, that others realize that good information skills have value in a broad range of roles in any organization. They are willing to take librarians out of the library, transfer their skills to new technology, integrate them into work teams, give them opportunities to stretch as information professionals, and maximize their contribution to any organization with a rich information culture.

LITERATURE CITED

1. Heath Row, "Out of the Stacks . . .", *CIO* 10 no.7 (15 January 1997), 59.
2. Ibid., 54-59.
3. Wendy Bukowitz, "In the Know," *CIO* 9, no. 12 (1 April 1996).
4. Heather Pemberton, "Online User Profile," *Online User* 2, no. 4 (July/August 1996), 37-42.
5. Anne Stuart, "Click & Dagger," *Webmaster* 1, no. 2 (July/August 1996), 38-43.
6. Cynthia N. James-Catalano, "Look to the Librarians," *Internet* World 7, no. 8 (August 1996), 28-30.
7. Amy M. DeBrower and Robert F. Skinder, "Designing an Internet Class for a Scientific and Technical Audience," *Special Libraries* 87, no. 3 (Summer 1996), 139-146.
8. Rick Tetzeli, "Getting Your Company's Internet Strategy Right," *Fortune* 133, no. 5 (18 March 1996), 73-78.
9. Mary Holland and Janell Picard, "Librarians at the Gate," *Webmaster* 1, no. 3 (September 1996), 22-26.
10. Tom Field, "Getting in Touch With Your Inner Web," *CIO* 10, no. 7 (15 January 1997), 38-44.
11. Christopher Koch, "Authors, Authors Everywhere," *Webmaster* 1, no. 7 (January 1997), 36-40.
12. Leigh Buchanan, "Internal Combustion," *WebMaster* (November/December 1995), 28-36. (Supplement to CIO Magazine.)
13. "PCA Health Plans' Barbara Denton: Don't Miss The Chance to 'Stretch' Your Career," *OPENDialog* (August 1996), 5.
14. Leigh Buchanan, "The Medium and the Message," *CIO* 8, no. 18 (July 1995), 75.
15. "PCA Health Plans' Barbara Denton: Don't Miss The Chance to 'Stretch' Your Career," *OPENDialog* (August 1996), 5.
16. Gitelle Seer, "Librarians Can Assist in Marketing Strategies," *New York Law Journal* (10 July 1995): S1.
17. Peggy Barber, "Public Relations Work," in *New Options for Librarians: Finding a Job in a Related Field,* ed. Betty-Carol Sellen and Dimity S. Berkner (New York: Neal-Schuman Publishers, 1984), 236-249.

18. Tom Davenport, "The Future of Knowledge Management," *CIO* 9, no. 6 (15 December/1 January 1996), 30-32.
19. Ibid.

FURTHER READING

Davenport, Tom and Larry Prusak. "Blow Up the Corporate Library." *International Journal of Information Management* 13 (1993), 405-412.

Garoogian, Rhoda and Andrew, Garoogian. *Careers in Other Fields For Librarians.* Chicago: American Library Association, 1985.

Hartel, Helen. "Knowledge Navigation or Why I Taught Tango Lessons." *Information Outlook* 1, no. 1 (January 1997), 10-12.

Horton, Forest W. *Extending the Librarian's Domain: A Survey of Emerging Occupations for Librarians and Information Professionals.* Washington, DC: Special Libraries Association, 1994.

Mount, Ellis. *Opening New Doors: Alternative Careers for Librarians.* Washington, DC: Special Libraries Association, 1993.

Sellen, Betty-Carol. *What Else You Can Do With a Library Degree.* Syracuse, NY: Gaylord Professional Publications, 1980.

Smith, Linda C. and Prudence W. Dalrymple. *Designing Information: New Roles for Librarians.* Urbana-Champaign, IL: Graduate School of Library and Information Science, University of Illinois at Urbana-Champaign, 1993.

APPENDIX

A

Glossary

abstracting: summarizing the content or conclusions of a document in a concise fashion.

acquisitions: obtaining materials for the library collection, including selection, ordering, invoicing, and receiving.

benchmarking: a management tool; measuring and comparing performance against a standard, often a best-in-class performer, within or outside the organization.

bibliographic networks: electronic cataloging records that are accessible to other organizations via established computer networks.

bibliography: list of materials, usually including author(s), title, publisher, and date.

call numbers: codes that describe the content of items (book, journal, tape, etc.) in a library in a general way; call numbers are alphabetical, numerical, or a combination of both, and are derived from classification systems such as the *Library of Congress Classification* or the *Dewey Decimal Classification System*.

cataloging: selecting appropriate subject terms to describe the content of an item.

CD-ROM: **C**ompact **D**isc—**R**ead **O**nly **M**emory; information etched onto a small optical disk.

change management: an organized approach to handling rapid changes within and beyond an organization, and responses to such changes.

classification scheme: an organized system for identifying materials by subject, author, or other means; classification schemes are used to create call numbers for materials.

competitive intelligence: a formalized process using information resources and primary research techniques to monitor an identified market in order to track trends and developments.

Copyright Clearance Center (CCC): a not-for-profit organization that provides copyright licenses to a wide range of applicants in order to assist them in complying with national copyright and permissions law.

collection: any materials, regardless of format, that make up the library's resources.

cross functional teams: an approach to tasks that involves staff from more than one functional area (e.g. accounting, customer service, etc.) working together.

current awareness services: any method of providing up-to-date information on an ongoing, scheduled basis.

cyberspace: slang for the collection of networks and resources that comprise the Internet, sometimes with special emphasis on the World Wide Web component; the term was coined by punk author William Gibson in his "cyberpunk" novel *Neuromancer*.

cybrarians: librarians whose primary role is to utilize Internet resources.

data: characters, numbers or other symbols that on their own do not have much meaning, but together create information that is meaningful; in order of hierarchy, data is the most elemental unit, followed by information, knowledge, understanding, and wisdom.

database: data that is organized so that it can be accessed and updated; a database is often in a tabular format, and usually consists of records comprised of fields; a library database typically has catalog records of books, with record fields including title, author(s), publisher, date published, etc.

desktop delivery service: news service that is available on an end user's personal computer or workstation.

document delivery or retrieval: method of obtaining documents or copies of articles from a fee-based service.

end user: usually refers to someone who performs their own searches on CD-ROM or online databases.

ephemera: materials of short-lived interest or physical construction (e.g., clippings, pamphlets).

format: a method of presenting (e.g., tabular, text, bulleted) and recording or preserving (e.g. printed book, CD-ROM, computer database file, etc.) information.

formula budget: a budget based on formula such as the library budget as a percentage of all administrative costs.

groupware: network software that enables communication and collaboration among workgroups without regard to the participants' physical location.

indexing: analyzing the contents of materials with references to topics, names, and other key elements therein.

information: a meaningful organization of data; in order of hierarchy, information is the second level, preceded by data and followed by knowledge, understanding, and wisdom.

information age: popular term for the current environment in which access to information is a key strategic asset.

information audit: a series of interviews with information consumers undertaken to determine the information needs of an organization and to inventory existing resources.

information function: organized effort by an organization to manage its information use and retrieval.

intellectual capital: the "brainpower" of all an organization's staff; realizing that staff members' knowledge is a resource for the organization.

interlibrary loan: method by which libraries share resources through formal or informal networks.

Internet: the global network of interconnected computer networks.

intranet: an organization's internal networked resources, especially in the form of web pages.

jobbers: agencies that manage the purchasing of books and journals to qualify for quantity discounts.

KWIC: **K**ey **W**ord **I**n **C**ontext; when a key word or search term is presented with the context in which it appears; in a KWIC document indexing system, each significant term in the title is used as a subject heading, with heading terms arranged in alphabetical sequence in a central column, with the remainder of the title arranged in its natural order around the index term.

KWOC: **K**ey **W**ord **O**ut of **C**ontext; similar to KWIC indexing except that the keywords are listed separately with the titles of the documents containing the keyword(s) listed below.

knowledge: information put to use; in order of hierarchy, knowledge is the third level, preceded by data, and information, and followed by understanding and wisdom.

knowledgebase: the collection of knowledge belonging to an organization.

knowledge culture: exists when an organization fosters the continuous use of its intellectual capital.

knowledge management: collecting and organizing the intellectual capital or knowledgebase of an organization in a manner that enables easy access to the information by others in the organization.

knowledge worker: an employee who interprets and perpetuates the knowledgebase of the organization for which he or she works.

library without walls: see virtual library.

line-item budget: a budget in which each expenditure is derived from the previous cycle's budget and categorized by line; each line is adjusted from the previous cycle per inflation or changing priorities.

lump-sum budget: a budget based on a lump-sum amount that is prioritized and divided by the manager.

mailing list: an informal networking facility in which e-mail from one member of an interest group can be sent to all other members of the group; distribution of members can be within an organization or worldwide on the Internet.

OCLC: the **O**n**l**ine **C**omputer **L**ibrary **C**enter in Dublin, Ohio; a cooperative cataloging resource and interlibrary loan system, as well as a vendor of various Internet and World Wide Web products such as electronic journals.

online searching: computer-based databases accessed and transmitted via telecommunications.

paradigm: the accepted, normal range of activities that support stated personal or professional methods and goals.

performance budget: a budget based on a cost-benefit analysis for each program or service being funded.

periodical: a publication such as a newspaper, magazine, or journal that is published at regular intervals and usually numbered in successive parts (volumes or issues); also referred to as a serial publication.

primary source material: original documents or studies developed for the purpose at hand.

program budget: a budget based on the programs or services being extended by the library; expenditures are linked to these programs or services.

reference interview: process by which the librarian discusses an information request with the user in order to gain insight or details needed to appropriately develop or focus a research strategy.

routing: the systematic distribution of current periodical issues to staff based on a predetermined need.

secondary source material: published materials that support the ideas of an author.

selection: choosing materials to address specific needs and criteria.

subject analysis: systems that lead a user to materials, or portions of them, based on subject.

stacks: the shelving units on which library materials are stored.

subject cataloging: selecting appropriate subject terms to reflect or describe the content of each item cataloged.

team environment: a management approach in which staff work together in teams to accomplish goals.

thesaurus, plural **thesauri**: a categorized list of terms, often presented in relationship to each other, e.g. broader and narrower terms in same topical area.

value-added: collection, editing, and analysis of information for delivery with the specific needs and preferences of the client in mind.

vertical file: a collection of clippings, pamphlets, and other miscellaneous materials usually stored in a filing cabinet and only minimally organized, often by subject.

virtual library: an information environment that relies largely on electronic sources, usually available at the user's desk top.

World Wide Web or the Web: Internet protocol using hypertext language to link documents together; usually employing graphics and other multimedia resources.

zero-based budget: a budget that starts from zero and builds the budget with necessary expenditures to support programs or services.

APPENDIX

B

Further Reading

The focus of the *Guide* has been on a broad outline of answers to the most frequently asked questions about special libraries. The titles in this highly selective list are generally characterized by a basic and practical approach to one or more aspects of the field. Readers with more specific or complex questions who want to read more extensively in an area of special librarianship covered in one of the chapters will want to look at the reading list at the end of that chapter.

Allan, Ferne C. "Benchmarking: Practical Aspects for Information Professionals." *Special Libraries* 84, no. 3 (Summer 1993): 123-130.

Anthony, L. J., ed. *Handbook of Special Librarianship and Information Work*, 5th ed. London: ASLIB, 1982.

Ardis, Susan B. *Library Without Walls: Plug in and Go*. Washington, DC: Special Libraries Association, 1994.

Asantewa, Doris. *Strategic Planning Basics for Special Libraries*. Washington, DC: Special Libraries Association, 1992.

Baker, Sharon L., and F. Wilfrid Lancaster. *The Measurement and Evaluation of Library Services*, 2nd ed. Arlington: Information Resources Press, 1991.

Berkman, Robert Irving. *Rethinking the Corporate Information Center: A Blueprint for the 21st Century*. New York: FIND/SVP, Inc., 1995.

Brimsek, Tobi A., ed. *From the Top: Profiles of U. S. and Canadian Corporate Libraries and Information Centers*. Washington, DC: Special Libraries Association, 1989.

Brooking, Annie. *Intellectual Capital*. London: International Thomson Publishing, Inc., 1996.

Christianson, Elin B., ed. *New Special Libraries: A Summary of Research*. New York: Special Libraries Association, 1980.

Darling, Louise, ed. *Handbook of Medical Library Practice*. 4th ed. 3 vols. Chicago: Medical Library Association, 1982-88. .

Davenport, Tom H., and Larry Prusak. "Blow Up the Corporate Library." *International Journal of Information Management* 13 (1993): 405-412.

Feeney, Mary and Maureen Grieves, eds. *The Value and Impact of Information*. London: Bowker-Saur, 1994.

Ferguson, Elizabeth, and Emily R. Mobley. *Special Libraries at Work*. Hamden, CT: Library Professional Publications, 1984.

Gasaway, Laura, and Sarah K. Wiant. *Libraries and Copyright: A Guide to Copyright Law in the 1990s*. Washington, DC: Special Libraries Association, 1994.

Griffiths, Jose-Marie, and Donald W. King. *Special Libraries: Increasing the Information Edge*. Washington, DC: Special Libraries Association, 1993.

Inside Information: Profiles of Association Libraries and Information Centers. Washington, DC: Special Libraries Association, 1991.

Koenig, Michael E. D. "Information Services and Downstream Productivity." In *Annual Review of Information Science and Technology*. Vol. 25. Amsterdam and New York: Elsevier, 1990.

Marshall, Joanne G. *The Impact of the Special Library on Corporate Decision-Making*. Washington, DC: Special Libraries Association, 1993.

Matarazzo, James M. *Corporate Library Excellence*. Washington, DC: Special Libraries Association, 1990.

Matarazzo, James M., and Miriam A. Drake. *Information for Management: A Handbook*. Washington, DC: Special Libraries Association, 1994.

Matarazzo, James M., and Laurence Pruzak. *The Value of Corporate Libraries: Findings from a 1995 Survey of Senior Management*. Washington, DC: Special Libraries Association, 1995.

Matarazzo, James, Laurence Pruzak, and Michael R. Gauthier. *Valuing Corporate Libraries: A Survey of Senior Managers*. Washington, DC: Special Libraries Association, 1990.

Mount, Ellis. *Special Libraries and Information Centers: An Introductory Text*, 3rd ed. Washington, DC: Special Libraries Association, 1995.

Owens, Ian, Tom Wilson, and Angela Abell. *Information and Business Performance: A Study of Information Systems and Services in High Performing Companies*. London: Bowker-Saur, 1996.

Pruett, Nancy Jones. *Scientific and Technical Libraries*. 2 vols. Orlando, FL: Academic Press, 1986.

Prusak, Laurence, and James Matarazzo. *Information Management and Japanese Success*. Washington, DC: Special Libraries Association, 1992.

Remeikis, Lois. "Learning Organizations and Knowledge Management: A Bibliography Compiled by Lois Remeikis." *Library Management Quarterly* 18, no. 4 (Fall 1995): 5-6.

Saunders, Laverna, ed. *The Evolving Virtual Library: Visions and Case Studies.* Medford, NJ: Information Today, Inc., 1996.

Schlessinger, Bernard S., ed. *The Basic Business Library: Core Resources*. 3rd ed. Phoenix: Oryx Press, 1995.

Smith, Linda C., and Prudence W. Dalrymple. *Designing Information: New Roles for Librarians*. Urbana-Champaign, IL: University of Illinois Graduate School of Library and Information Science, 1993.

Special Libraries Association. *Final Report of the President's Task Force of the Value of the Information Professional*. Washington, DC: Special Libraries Association, 1987.

Special Libraries Association. *Objectives for Special Libraries*. New York: Special Libraries Association, 1964. (Single copies free on request.).

Special Libraries Association. *The Information Audit: An SLA Information Kit.* Washington, DC: Special Libraries Association, 1995.

Special Libraries Association. *The Virtual Library: An SLA Information Kit.* Washington, DC: Special Libraries Association, 1994.

Special Libraries Association. *Valuing Special Libraries and Information Centers: An SLA Information Kit.* Washington, DC: Special Libraries Association, 1993.

St. Clair, Guy. *Customer Service in the Information Environment*. London: Bowker-Saur, 1993.

St. Clair, Guy. *Entrepreneurial Librarianship: The Key to Effective Information Services Management*. London: Bowker-Saur, 1996.

St. Clair, Guy. *Power and Influence: Enhancing Information Services Within the Organization*. London: Bowker-Saur, 1994.

St. Clair, Guy and Joan Williamson. *Managing the* New *One-Person Library*. London: Bowker-Saur, 1992.

Stewart, Thomas A. "Your Company's Most Valuable Asset: Intellectual Capital." *Fortune* 130, no. 7 (3 October 1994): 68-74.

White, Herbert S. "The Perilous But Also Opportune Future For Special Librarians." *Library Journal* (January 1996): 59-60.

APPENDIX

C

ALA Accredited Library and Information Science Master's Programs in the United States and Canada

This list is compiled by the American Library Association and can be viewed on their homepage at http://www.ala.org/alaorg/oa/uslis.html (United States schools) and http://www.ala.org/alaorg/oa/canlis.html (Canadian schools).

UNITED STATES

ALABAMA

The University of Alabama, School of Library and Information Studies
Box 870252, Tuscaloosa, AL 35487-0252
Phone: 205-348-4610, Fax: 205-348-3746
Philip M. Turner, Dean, pturner@ualvsm.ua.edu

ARIZONA

University of Arizona, School of Library Science
1515 E. First Street, Tucson, AZ 85719
Phone: 520-621-3566, Fax: 520-621-3279
ualibsci@ccit.arizona.edu, http://www.sir.arizona.edu
Charlie D. Hurt, Director

CALIFORNIA

San Jose State University, School of Library and Information Science
One Washington Square, San Jose, CA 95192-0029
Phone: 408-924-2490, Fax: 408-924-2476
office@wahoo.sjsu.edu
Stuart A. Sutton, Director

University of California, Los Angeles, Department of Library and Information Science, Graduate School of Education and Information Studies
2320 Moore Hall, Mailbox 951521, Los Angeles, CA 90095-1521
Phone: 310-825-8799, Fax: 310-206-3076 or 4460
http://www.gslis.ucla.edu/LIS/
Christine L. Borgman, Chair, cborgman@ucla.edu

CONNECTICUT

Southern Connecticut State University, School of Communication, Information and Library Science
501 Crescent Street, New Haven, CT 06515
Phone: 203-392-5781, Fax: 203-392-5780
libscienceit@scsu.ctstateu.edu
Edward C. Harris, Dean

DISTRICT OF COLUMBIA

The Catholic University of America, School of Library and Information Science
Washington, D.C. 20064
Phone: 202-319-5085, Fax: 202-319-5574
Elizabeth Aversa, Dean, aversa@cua.edu

FLORIDA

Florida State University, School of Library and Information Studies
Tallahassee, FL 32306-2048
Phone: 904-644-5775, Fax: 904-644-9763
Jane B. Robbins, Dean

University of South Florida, School of Library and Information Science
4202 East Fowler Avenue, CIS 1040, Tampa, FL 33620-7800
Phone: 813-974-3520, Fax: 813-974-6840
epate@cis01.cis.usf.edu, http://www.cas.usf.edu/lis/index.html
Kathleen de la Pena McCook, Director

GEORGIA

Clark Atlanta University, School of Library and Information Studies
300 Trevor Arnett Hall, James P. Brawley Drive
@ Fair Street, Atlanta, GA 30314
Phone: 404-880-8695, Fax: 404-880-8395
Charles D. Churchwell, Dean

HAWAII

University of Hawaii, School of Library and Information Studies
2550 The Mall, Honolulu, HI 96822
Phone: 808-956-7321, Fax: 808-956-5835
Miles M. Jackson, Dean and Professor, jackson@uhunix.uhcc.hawaii.edu

ILLINOIS

Rosary College, Graduate School of Library and Information Science
7900 W. Division Street, River Forest, IL 60305
Phone: 708-524-6845, Fax: 708-524-6657
Peggy Sullivan, Dean, sullivan@email.rosary.edu

University of Illlinois at Urbana-Champaign, Graduate School of Library and Information Science
Library and Information Science Building, 501 East Daniel Street, Champaign, Illinois 61820
Phone: 217-333-3280, Fax: 217-244-3302
http://alexia.lis.uiuc.edu
Leigh S. Estabrook, Dean

INDIANA

Indiana University, School of Library and Information Science
Library 011, Bloomington, IN 47405-1801
Phone: 812-855-2018, Fax: 812-855-6166
iuslis@indiana.edu, http://www-slis.lib.indiana.edu
Blaise Cronin, Dean/Professor of Information Science

IOWA

University of Iowa, School of Library and Information Science
3087 Library, The University of Iowa, Iowa City, IA 52242-1420
Phone: 319-335-5707, Fax: 319-335-5374
http://www.uiowa.edu/~libsci
Carl F. Orgren, Director, carl-orgren@uiowa.edu

KANSAS

Emporia State University, School of Library and Information Management
PO Box 4025, Emporia, KS 66801
Phone: 316-341-5203, Fax: 316-341-5233
http://www.emporia.edu/S/www/slim/slim.htm
Faye Vowell, Dean

KENTUCKY

University of Kentucky, College of Communications
and Information Studies, School of Library and Information Science
502 King Library Building S, Lexington, KY 40506-0039
Phone: 606-257-8876, Fax: 606-257-4205
http://www.uky.edu/CommInfoStudies/SLIS/
Donald O. Case, Director, dcase@ukcc.uky.edu

LOUISIANA

Louisiana State University, School of Library and Information Science
267 Coates Hall, Baton Rouge, LA 70803
Phone: 504-388-3158, Fax: 504-388-4581
lsslis@lsuvm.sncc.lsu.edu
Bert R. Boyce, Dean

MARYLAND

University of Maryland, College of Library and Information Services
4105 Hornbake Library Building, College Park, MD 20742-4345
Phone: 301-405-2033, Fax: 301-314-9145
Ann E. Prentice, Dean, ap57@umail.umd.edu

MASSACHUSETTS

Simmons College, Graduate School of Library and Information Science
300 The Fenway, Boston, MA 02115-5898
Phone: 617-521-2800, Fax: 617-521-3192
sknowles@vmsvax.simmons.edu
James M. Matarazzo, Dean and Professor

MICHIGAN

University of Michigan, School of Information and Library Studies
West Engineering, 550 E. University Avenue,
Ann Arbor, MI 48109-1092
Phone: 313-763-2285, Fax: 313-764-2475
sils.admissions@umich.edu, http://www.sils.umich.edu
Daniel E. Atkins, Dean

Wayne State University, Library and Information Science Program
106 Kresge Library, Detroit, MI 48202
Phone: 313-577-1825, Fax: 313-577-7563
info@lisp.purdy.wayne.edu, http://www.libraries.wayne.edu/LISP/lishome.html
Robert P. Holley, Director

MISSISSIPPI

University of Southern Mississippi, School of Library and Information Science
Box 5146, Hattiesburg, MS 39406-5146
Phone: 601-266-4228, Fax: 601-266-5774
Joy M. Greiner, Director

MISSOURI

University of Missouri-Columbia, School of Library and Informational Science
104 Stewart Hall, Columbia, MO 65211
Phone: 314-882-4546, Fax: 314-884-4944
http://www.slis.missouri.edu
Mary F. Lenox, Dean

NEW JERSEY

Rutgers University, School of Communication,
Information and Library Studies
4 Huntington Street, New Brunswick, NJ 08901-1071
Phone: 908-932-7500, Fax: 908-932-6916
Richard W. Budd, Dean, budd@zodiac.rutgers.edu

NEW YORK

Long Island University, Palmer School of Library and Information Science
C. W. Post Campus, 720 Northern Blvd., Brookville, NY 11548-1300
Phone: 516-299-2866, Fax: 516-299-4168
palmer@aurora.liunet.edu
Anne Woodsworth, Dean

Pratt Institute, School of Information and Library Science
Information Science Center, 200 Willoughby Avenue,
Brooklyn, NY 11205
Phone: 718-636-3702, Fax: 718-636-3733
sils@acnet.pratt.edu
S. M. Matta, Dean

Queens College, City University of New York,
Graduate School of Library and Information Studies
65-30 Kissena Blvd., Flushing, NY 11367
Phone: 718-997-3790, Fax: 718-997-3797
Marianne Cooper, Director

St. John's University, Division of Library and Information Science
8000 Utopia Parkway, Jamaica, NY 11439
Phone: 718-990-6200, Fax: 718-380-0353
libis@sjumusic.stjohns.edu
James A. Benson, Director

Syracuse University, School of Information Studies
4-206 Center for Science and Technology, Syracuse, NY 13244-4100
Phone: 315-443-2911, Fax: 315-443-5806
http://istweb.syr.edu
Raymond F. von Dran, Dean, vondran@syr.edu

University at Albany, State University of New York, School of Information
Science and Policy
135 Western Avenue, Draper 113, Albany, NY 12222
Phone: 518-442-5110, Fax: 518-442-5232
infosci@cnsvax.albany.edu
Philip B. Eppard, Interim Dean

University at Buffalo, School of Information and Library Studies
381 Baldy Hall, Buffalo, NY 14260-1020
Phone: 716-645-2412, Fax: 716-645-3775
sils@ubvms.cc.buffalo.edu
George S. Bobinski, Dean

NORTH CAROLINA

North Carolina Central University, School of Library
and Information Sciences
PO Box 19586, Durham, NC 27707
Phone: 919-560-6485, Fax: 919-560-6402
Benjamin F. Speller, Jr., Dean, speller@ecsvax.uncecs.edu

University of North Carolina at Chapel Hill,
School of Information and Library Science
CB #3360 100 Manning Hall, Chapel Hill, SC 27599-3360
Phone: 919-962-8366, Fax: 919-962-8071
info@ils.unc.edu, http://ils.unc.edu/ilshome.html
Barbara B. Moran, Dean and Professor

The University of North Carolina at Greensboro,
Department of Library and Information Studies
349 Curry Building, Greensboro, NC 27412-5001
Phone: 910-334-3477, Fax: 910-334-5060
meeksl@iris.uncg.edu, http://www.uncg.edu/lis/
Marilyn L. Miller, Chair

OHIO

Kent State University, School of Library and Information Science
Room 314 KSU Library, PO Box 5190, Kent, OH 44242-0001
Phone: 216-672-2782, Fax: 216-672-7965
http://phoenix.kent.edu/~slis
Danny Wallace, Director

OKLAHOMA

University of Oklahoma, School of Library and Information Studies
401 W. Brooks, Room 120, Norman, OK 73019-0528
Phone: 405-325-3921, Fax: 405-325-7648
slisinfo@uoknor.edu, http://www.uoknor.edu/cas/slis
June Lester, Director

PENNSYLVANIA

Clarion University of Pennsylvania, College of Communication, Computer
Information Science and Library Science
109 Becker Hall, Clarion, PA 16214
Phone: 814-226-2328, Fax: 814-226-2186
Rita Rice Flaningam, Dean, flaninga@vaxa.clarion.edu

Drexel University, College of Information Science and Technology
3141 Chestnut Street, Philadelphia, PA 19104
Phone: 215-895-2474, Fax: 215-895-2494
http://www.cis.drexel.edu
Richard H. Lytle, Dean

University of Pittsburgh, School of Library and Information Science
505 SLIS Building, Pittsburgh, PA 15260
Phone: 412-624-5230, Fax: 412-624-5231
http://www.lis.pitt.edu
Toni Carbo Bearman, Dean and Professor

PUERTO RICO

University of Puerto Rico, Graduate School of Library and Information Science
PO Box 21906, San Juan, Puerto Rico 00931-1906
Phone: 809-763-6199, Fax: 809-764-2311
Mariano A. Maura, Director, m_maura@uprl.upr.clu.edu

RHODE ISLAND

University of Rhode Island, Graduate School of Library and Information Studies
Rodman Hall, Kingston, RI 02881
Phone: 401-792-2947, Fax: 401-792-4395
Jonathan S. Tryon, Director

SOUTH CAROLINA

University of South Carolina, College of Library and Information Science
Davis College, Columbia, SC 29208
Phone: 803-777-3858, Fax: 803-777-7938
http://www.libsci.scarolina.edu/
Fred W. Roper, Dean

TENNESSEE

University of Tennessee, School of Information Sciences
804 Volunteer Blvd., Knoxville, TN 37996-4330
Phone: 423-974-2148, Fax: 423-974-4967
http://pepper.lis.utk.edu
Jose-Marie Griffiths, Director

TEXAS

Texas Woman's University, School of Library and Information Studies
PO Box 425438, Denton, TX 76204-3438
Phone: 817-898-2602, Fax: 817-898-2611
Keith Swigger, Dean, a_swigger@twu.edu

University of North Texas, School of Library and Information Sciences
PO Box 13796, NT Station, Denton, TX 76203
Phone: 817-565-2445, Fax: 817-565-3101
slis@unt.edu, http://www-lan.unt.edu/slis/
James Miller, Interim Dean

The University of Texas at Austin, Graduate School of Library and Information Science
Austin, TX 78712-1276
Phone: 512-471-3821, Fax: 512-471-3971
gslis@uts.cc.utexas.edu, http://fiat.gslis.utexas.edu
Brooke E. Sheldon, Dean

WASHINGTON

University of Washington, Graduate School of Library and Information Science
133 Suzzallo Library, Box 352930, Seattle, WA 98195-2930
Phone: 206-543-1794, Fax: 206-616-3152
http://weber.u.washington.edu/~gslis
Phyllis Van Orden, Director and Professor

WISCONSIN

University of Wisconsin-Madison, School of Library and Information Studies
Helen C. White Hall, 600 N. Park Street, Madison, WI 53706
Phone: 608-263-2900, Fax: 608-263-4849
uw.slis@doit.wisc.edu
James Krikelas, Interim Director

University of Wisconsin-Milwaukee, School of Library and Information Science
Enderis Hall 1110, 2400 E. Hartford Avenue, Milwaukee, WI 53211
Phone: 414-229-4707, Fax: 414-229-4848
http://www.uwm.edu/Dept/SLIS
Mohammed M. Aman, Dean, aman@csd.uwm.edu

CANADA

ALBERTA

University of Alberta, School of Library and Information Studies
3-20 Rutherford South, Edmonton, AB, Canada T6G 2J4
Phone: 403-492-4578, Fax: 403-492-2430
office@slis.ualberta.ca
Sheila Bertram, Director

BRITISH COLUMBIA

The University of British Columbia, School of Library, Archival and Information Studies
1956 Main Mall, Rm. 831, Vancouver, BC, Canada V6T 1Z1
Phone: 604-822-2404, Fax: 604-822-6006
slais@unixg.ubc.ca, http://edziza.arts.ubc.ca/slais/slaisa.html
Ken Haycock, Director

ONTARIO

University of Toronto, Faculty of Information Studies
140 St. George Street, Toronto, ON, Canada M5S 1A1
Phone: 416-978-8589, Fax: 416-978-5762
http://www.fis.utoronto.ca
Lynne C. Howarth, Dean

The University of Western Ontario, Graduate School of Library and Information Science
Elborn College, London, ON, Canada N6G 1H1
Phone: 519-661-3542, Fax: 519-661-3506
Jean Tague-Sutcliffe, Dean, tague@julian.uwo.ca

NOVA SCOTIA

Dalhousie University, School of Library and Information Studies
Faculty of Management, Halifax, NS, Canada B3H 3J5
Phone: 902-494-3656, Fax: 902-494-2451
slis@ac.dal.ca, http://quasar.sba.dal.ca:2000/slis/slis.html
Bertrum H. MacDonald, Director

QUEBEC

McGill University, Graduate School of Library and Information Studies
3459 McTavish Street, Montreal, QB, Canada H3A 1Y1
Phone: 514-398-4204, Fax: 514-398-7193
ad27@musica.mcgill.ca, http://www.gslis.mcgill.ca
J. Andrew Large, Director

Universite de Montreal, Ecole de bibliotheconomie et des sciences de l'information
C.P. 6128, Succursale Centre-Ville, Montreal, Quebec, Canada H3C 3J7
Phone: 514-343-6044, Fax: 514-343-5753
http://tornade.ere.umontreal.ca/~carmellu/ebsi
Gilles Deschatelets, Directeur, deschatg@ere.umontreal.ca

APPENDIX

D

Professional Associations

Below is a partial list of professional associations to which special librarians belong. Most of these organizations also have local or regional chapters that meet regularly; contact information can be obtained from the national offices listed below. Consulting and recruiting services are sometimes available at both the regional and national levels. All have annual conferences that many special librarians attend, and many offer professional development courses.

American Association of Law Libraries (AALL)
53 West Jackson Boulevard, Suite 940
Chicago, IL 60604
312-939-4764
http://lawlib.wuacc.edu/aallnet/aallnet.html

American Library Association (ALA)
50 East Huron Street
Chicago, IL 60611
312-944-6780
http://www.ala.org/

American Society for Information Science (ASIS)
8720 Georgia Avenue, Suite 501
Silver Spring, MD 20910-3602
301-495-0900
http://www.asis.org/

Association of College and Research Libraries (ACRL)
50 East Huron Street
Chicago, IL 60611-2795
312-280-3248
http://www.ala.org/acrl.html

Association of Records Managers and Administrators (ARMA)
4200 Somerset, Suite 215
Prairie Village, KS 66208
913-341-3808
http://www.arma.org/hq/

Association of Research Libraries (ARL)
21 Dupont Circle, NW
Washington, DC 20036
202-296-2296
http://arl.cni.org/

Canadian Association for Information Science
CAIS Secretariat
University of Toronto
140 St. George Street
Toronto, Ontario M5S 3G6
416-978-8876

Canadian Library Association (CLA)
200 Elgin Street, Suite 602
Ottawa, Ontario K2P 1L5
613-232-9625
http://www.ncf.carleton.ca/freeport/prof.assoc/cla/menu

Medical Library Association (MLA)
6 North Michigan Avenue, Suite 300
Chicago, IL 60602-4805
312-419-9094
http://www.kumc.edu/MLA/

Society of American Archivists (SAA)
600 South Federal Street, Suite 504
Chicago, IL 60605
312-922-0140
http://volvo.gslis.utexas.edu/~us-saa/index.html

Society of Competitive Intelligence Professionals (SCIP)
1700 Diagonal Road, Suite 520
Alexandria, VA 22314
703-739-0696
http://www.scip.org/homepage.html

Special Libraries Association (SLA)
1700 Eighteenth Street, NW
Washington, DC 20009-2508
202-234-4700
http://www.sla.org/

APPENDIX

E

Competencies for Special Librarians of the 21st Century

FULL REPORT—MAY 1996

Special Committee on Competencies for Special Librarians
Joanne Marshall, Chair; Bill Fisher; Lynda Moulton; Roberta Piccoli

BACKGROUND TO THE DOCUMENT

The Special Libraries Association (SLA), an organization of dynamic and change-oriented information professionals, has long been interested in the knowledge requirements of new entrants to the field. The Association's members have explored and shared their vision of the competencies and skills required for special librarianship in many forums over the years as shown by the accompanying bibliography. This document is an attempt to synthesize and build upon this earlier work in the light of the rapid social, technological, and workplace transformations that are taking place.

Competencies have been defined as the interplay of knowledge, understanding, skills and attitudes required to do a job effectively from the point of view of both the performer and the observer (Murphy, 1991). *The unique competencies of the special librarian include in-depth knowledge of print and electronic information resources in specialized subject areas and the design and management of information services that meet the strategic information needs of the individual or group being served.*

In personal career development terms, competencies can also be thought of as flexible knowledge and skills that allow the special librarian to function in a variety of environments and to produce a continuum of value-added, customized information services that cannot be easily duplicated by others. At a time when professionals in all fields are being encouraged to invest in themselves and to prepare for employment as independent contractors, it is critical that special librarians define their unique competencies and that they continue to improve the range of professional and personal competencies that will form the basis for their future careers.

THE AUDIENCE

The primary audience for previous SLA documents on competencies has been library and information studies (LIS) educators. The need for communication between professional groups such as SLA and LIS educators is supported in the American Library Association (1992) guidelines for the accreditation of Masters' programs in library and information studies. Such communication can foster the development of curricula that respond to the needs and demands of the real world of information work. There is also a wider audience for this document. *Prospective students* who are considering special librarianship as a career can use this document as a guide to the content and approaches that they should look for in a LIS curriculum. As proactive lifelong learners, *currently practicing special librarians* will also find the competencies useful as a framework for defining their own professional development and continuing education needs.

Last, and of key importance, *managers who are responsible for hiring library and information professionals* as full-time employees, contract employees or as information brokers can use this document to inform themselves about the knowledge and skills of special librarians and the value that they add to the organization or to the particular task at hand.

THE ENVIRONMENT

As we move towards the millennium, library and information professionals are facing at least three major paradigm shifts.

- The first shift is the *transition from paper to electronic media* as the dominant form of information storage and retrieval. Linked to this transition is the convergence of previously separate media, such as text, graphics, and sound, into multimedia resources.
- The second shift relates to the *increasing demand for accountability*, including a focus on customers, performance measurement, bench marking and continuous improvement. All of this is taking place in an era when the financial resources available for providing library and information services are shrinking.
- The third shift comes from *new forms of work organization* such as end-user computing, work teams, management delayering, job sharing, telework, outsourcing, downsizing, and re-engineering.

All three of these shifts are related to a combination of factors such as global competition, new computing and communications technologies, and the perceived need to measure the productivity of knowledge and service workers.

We are facing these paradigm shifts at a time when the workforce is aging and when we as a profession are aging. In the year 2000, the average age of the worker in the United States will be 39 and this will increase until the last of the baby boom generation has reached retirement age in 2031 (Johnston and Packer, 1987, p.81). In an earlier era, we might have looked for innovation and change to come from increasing numbers of new entrants to the field of special librarianship; however, the demographics and the current economic situation have determined that those of us who are currently in the field must continue to play a vital and active role. This is why this document on competencies is addressed to both new entrants and practicing special librarians—we must all learn and change together if we are to reach our full potential as information professionals in the information age. We must also communicate the broad range of competencies held by special librarians to current and prospective employers.

The changing landscape suggests that a document on competencies of special librarians produced in 1996 will necessarily take a different shape from those produced in earlier times when resources were more plentiful and change was proceeding at a slower pace. A document produced by SLA must also take into account the particular environments in which special librarians work. There are close to 15,000 members of SLA and almost 60% are employed in small libraries with six or fewer staff. Solo librarians are estimated to make up 30% to 50% of the membership and over half of the members work in corporate business settings. Increasing numbers of librarians are working as independent information brokers or in contract positions. In comparison to their colleagues in academic and public libraries, special librarians frequently work in settings without professional peers. As a result, special librarians must often work harder than librarians in other settings to make themselves recognizable and to align themselves with the strategic direction of the organization. Just as organizations are refocusing on their core competencies in response to global competition, it is time for special librarians to take a fresh look at what they do best and to reaffirm their commitment to continuing competence and growth.

THE VALUE OF THE SPECIAL LIBRARIAN

The special librarian adds value by providing efficient and effective information services for a defined group of customers. The special librarian may be a full-time member of an information management team in an organization or hired on a part-time or contract basis for special projects. The unique contributions of the special librarian include expertise in the content and selection of the best available print and electronic information resources as well as a commitment to putting knowledge to work or, in other words, linking the information user with the right information resource at the right time.

The special librarian understands the critical role that information plays for organizations and for individuals and takes a holistic view of information needs and uses and the contexts in which they occur. The special librarian identifies, retrieves, organizes, repackages, and presents information in an actionable form so that the potential for goal attainment is maximized. The special librarian helps control the flood of available information by selecting what is relevant and usable and, when required, analyzing or synthesizing the content.

The special librarian is a technology application leader who works with other members of the information management team to design and evaluate systems for information access that meet user needs. Where required, the special librarian provides instruction and support so that end users can make optimal use of the information resources available to them. The special librarian is capable of working in the hybrid world of print and electronic media and providing the best mix of information resources in the most appropriate formats for the environment.

The special librarian plays a key role in developing information policy for the organization ensuring that access to all information resources— from internal records to external databases—is provided in the most strategically-effective and cost-effective manner. The special librarian also plays another important role in ensuring that contractual, legal, and ethical obligations regarding information use are met. The electronic information age provides new opportunities for organizations to produce as well as use information products. Special librarians, given their familiarity with the information marketplace, can be key contributors to the development, marketing and use of information products.

Special librarians are knowledge-based practitioners who use research as a foundation for their own professional practice and who support the conduct of research through their professional associations such as SLA. Research has shown that the provision of appropriate information can lead to: better-informed decision-making; the ability to proceed to the next step in a project or task; improved relations with a client; and the exploitation of new business opportunities. The right information at the right time can also benefit the organization by saving the time of highly paid employees, avoiding poor business decisions, and even direct loss of funds (Marshall, 1993).

In the information age, special librarians are essential—by responding with a sense of urgency to critical information needs they provide the information edge for the knowledge-based organization. In order to fulfill this key information role, special librarians require two main types of competencies:

- *Professional competencies* relate to the special librarian's knowledge in the areas of information resources, information access, technology, management and research, and the ability to use these areas of knowledge as a basis for providing library and information services.

- *Personal competencies* represent a set of skills, attitudes, and values that enable librarians to work efficiently; be good communicators; focus on continuing learning throughout their careers; demonstrate the value-added nature of their contributions; and survive in the new world of work.

The following sections highlight the major professional and personal competencies of special librarians and provide practical examples of the multitude of roles and tasks that special librarians can perform.

1. PROFESSIONAL COMPETENCIES

The special librarian . . .

1.1 has expert knowledge of the content of information resources, including the ability to critically evaluate and filter them.

Practical examples: Evaluates print, CD-ROM, and online versions of databases. Knows "the best" textbooks, journals, and electronic resources in specific areas such as biology, marketing, or accounting. Evaluates and selects key information resources, print and electronic, for a small research center. Sets up a desktop news wire service for a petrochemical company. Controls the over supply of information by selecting what is relevant and usable for the customer. Uses strategic thinking to perform information selection and analysis that meets specific organizational goals.

1.2 has specialized subject knowledge appropriate to the business of the organization or client.

Practical examples: In addition to their Masters degree in library and information studies, many special librarians have subject degrees at the undergraduate and postgraduate levels. Librarians frequently take additional courses in finance, management or other subjects related to their host organization. Maintains a view of the organization's business by reading core journals and other key sources. This enables the development of in-depth, subject specialty information services, including current awareness.

1.3 develops and manages convenient, accessible and cost-effective information services that are aligned with the strategic directions of the organization.

Practical examples: Develops a strategic plan linked to the business goals of the organization. Sets up effective management, supervision and budget processes. Builds an effective staff team to manage information services. Conducts intermediary searches for complex, difficult or multifoil searches. Obtains documents in print or electronic form. Builds a core in-house library collection. Analyzes and synthesizes information as required. Develops specialized thesauri and lists of indexing terms for databases.

1.4 provides excellent instruction and support for library and information service users.

Practical examples: Teaches Internet courses for employees. Develops specialized end user searching courses on information resources related to current business goals. Keeps up-to-date with latest training and instructional techniques. Provides trouble-shooting service for employees who are accessing information services from the desktop. Provides online reference and assistance.

1.5 assesses information needs and designs and markets value-added information services and products to meet identified needs.

Practical examples: Conducts regular needs assessments using research tools such as questionnaires, focus groups, and key informant interviews. Reports the results to management and demonstrates the relationship between needs and services provided. Identifies and meets information needs by becoming a member of project teams. Contributes unique or unusual needs assessment findings to the professional literature.

1.6 uses appropriate information technology to acquire, organize, and disseminate information.

Practical examples: Creates an online catalog of the library collection. Links catalog searching to a document delivery service. Works with the information management team to select appropriate software and hardware for desktop access to the library catalog and other databases. Provides a support service for electronic information service users. Keeps up-to-date with new electronic information products and modes of information delivery.

1.7 uses appropriate business and management approaches to communicate the importance of information services to senior management.

Practical examples: Develops a business plan for the library. Calculates a return on investment for the library and its services. Develops a marketing plan for the library. Conducts a bench marking study. Reports to management on continuous quality improvement efforts. Demonstrates how library and information services add value to the organization. Acts as a resource for the organization on quality management, including ISO 9000 certification.

1.8 develops specialized information products for use inside or outside the organization or by individual clients.

Practical examples: Creates databases of in-house documents such as reports, technical manuals or resource materials used for special projects. Creates searchable full-text document files. Mounts online technical manuals created in-house. Creates a home page on the World Wide Web for the organization. Links the home page to other sites of interest on the Internet. Participates in knowledge management activities that create, capture, exchange, use and communicate the organization's "intellectual capital" (Remeikis, 1996).

1.9 evaluates the outcomes of information use and conducts research related to the solution of information management problems.

Practical examples: Gathers data related to needs assessment, program planning, and evaluation. Develops measures of frequency of use of services, customer satisfaction, and impact of information on organizational decision-making. Actively seeks opportunities for improvement and strives to be the best-in-class on key services such as current awareness, reference and resource sharing. Participates in research projects.

1.10 continually improves information services in response to the changing needs.

Practical examples: Monitors industry trends and disseminates information to key people in the organization or to individual clients. Refocuses information services on new business needs. Uses just-in-time document delivery to retain maximum flexibility. Monitors purchases of information products by departments to ensure that they are cost effective and aligned with current business needs.

1.11 is an effective member of the senior management team and a consultant to the organization on information issues.

Practical examples: Participates in strategic planning in the organization. Participates in bench marking or re-engineering teams. Informs management on copyright issues and monitors compliance with copyright law. Negotiates contracts with database vendors. Obtains patent information. Develops information policies for the organization.

2. PERSONAL COMPETENCIES

The special librarian...

2.1 is committed to service excellence.

Practical examples: Seeks out performance feedback and uses it for continuous improvement. Conducts regular user surveys. Asks library users if they found what they were looking for. Celebrates own success and that of others. Takes pride in a job well done. Shares new knowledge with others at conferences and in the professional literature. Uses the research knowledge base of special librarianship as a resource for improving services.

2.2 seeks out challenges and sees new opportunities both inside and outside the library.

Practical examples: Takes on new roles in the organization that require an information leader. Uses library-based knowledge and skills to solve a variety of information problems in a wide range of settings, both for individuals or for organizations. Does not limit the library collection or the information search to traditional media such as books and journals.

2.3 sees the big picture.

Practical examples: Recognizes that information-seeking and use is part of the creative process for individuals and for organizations. Sees the library and its information services as part of the bigger process of making informed decisions. Gives the highest priority to urgent demands that are critical to the organization's competitive advantage. Monitors major business trends and world events. Anticipates trends and pro-actively realigns library and information services to take advantage of them.

2.4 looks for partnerships and alliances.

Practical examples: Seeks alliances with management information systems (MIS) professionals to optimize complementary knowledge and skills. Provides leadership on the information management team. Forms partnerships with other libraries or information services inside or outside the organization to optimize resource sharing. Seeks alliances with database vendors and other information providers to improve products and services. Seeks alliances with researchers in faculties of library and information studies to conduct research.

2.5 creates an environment of mutual respect and trust.

Practical examples: Treats others with respect and expects to be treated with respect in return. Knows own strengths and the complementary strengths of others. Delivers on time and on target and expects others to do the same. Creates a problem-solving environment in which everyone's contribution is valued and acknowledged.

2.6 has effective communications skills.

Practical examples: Listens first and coaches staff and others to develop their own solutions. Supports and participates in mentorship programs and succession planning. Runs meetings effectively. Presents ideas clearly and enthusiastically. Writes clear and understandable text. Requests feedback on communications skills and uses it to make improvements.

2.7 works well with others in a team.

Practical examples: Learns about the wisdom of teams and seeks out opportunities for team participation. Takes on responsibility in teams both inside and outside the library. Mentors other team members. Asks for mentoring from others when it is needed. Constantly looks for ways to enhance own performance and that of others through formal and informal learning opportunities.

2.8 provides leadership.

Practical examples: Learns about and cultivates the qualities of a good leader and knows when to exercise leadership. Can share leadership with others or allow others to take the leadership role. Exercises leadership within the library and as a member of other teams or units within the organization. Acknowledges the contribution of all members of the team.

2.9 plans, prioritizes and focuses on what is critical.

Practical examples: Recognizes that in order to use resources most effectively, that ongoing, careful planning is required. Develops an approach to planning and time management that incorporates personal and professional goals. Reviews goals on a regular basis, prioritizes them, and makes sure that an appropriate proportion of daily activities are related to the most critical personal and professional goals. Mentors others to do the same.

2.10 is committed to lifelong learning and personal career planning.

Practical examples: Committed to a career that involves ongoing learning and knowledge development. Takes personal responsibility for long-term career planning and seeks opportunities for learning and enrichment. Advocates for an approach that encourages and supports ongoing knowledge development and that values the contribution of people. Maintains a strong sense of self-worth based on the achievement of a balanced set of evolving personal and professional goals.

2.11 has developed personal business skills and creates new opportunities.

Practical examples: Recognizes that, in the changing world or work, entrepreneurship and the ability to function as a small business professional are essential skills. Seeks out opportunities to develop these skills. Willing to take employment in a variety of forms including full-time, contract, and project work. Uses the entrepreneurial spirit in the organizational environment to revitalize products and services.

2.12 recognizes the value of professional networking and solidarity.

Practical examples: Active in SLA and other professional associations. Uses these opportunities to share knowledge and skills, to bench mark against other information service providers, and to form partnerships and alliances. Recognizes the need for a forum where information professionals can communicate with each other and speak with one voice on important information policy issues, such as copyright and the global information infrastructure.

2.13 is flexible and positive in a time of continuing change

Practical examples: Willing to take on different responsibilities at different points in time and to respond to changing needs. Maintains a positive attitude and helps others to do the same. Never says it cannot be done. Looks for solutions. Helps others to develop their new ideas by providing appropriate information. Always on the lookout for new ideas. Sees and uses technology as an enabler of new information ideas, products, and services.

CONCLUSION

These are the competencies for special librarians of the 21st century. They have their roots in the past, but they reach far into the future. Special librarians recognize the expanding nature of the challenges that face them in the information age and the range of competencies that are required to meet them. The challenges represented by these competencies must be seized and acted upon today in order to ensure that special librarians have a viable tomorrow.

The Special Committee on Competencies hopes that this document will evolve and grow through continuing discussion of our expanding base of knowledge and skills. We encourage SLA members to share additional practical examples of what they do with their competencies so that we can continue to learn from each other and celebrate our achievements. An Executive Summary of this document is available on the SLA website (www.sla.org) and a printed paper brochure from SLA headquarters (1-202-234-4700).

REFERENCES AND BIBLIOGRAPHY

Note: This list contains items that are cited in the document as well as background reading on the competencies of special librarians, the value of special libraries, and the changing nature of the field.

American Library Association. *Guidelines for the Accreditation of Master's Programs in Library and Information Studies.* Chicago: ALA, 1992.

Association for Library Collections and Technical Services (ALCTS) Educational Policy Statement. Chicago: ALA, 1995.

Bender, David R "Choosing Our Future." *Journal of Educational Media and Library Sciences* 30(4), summer 1993, 325-31.

Casey, Vicki. "Profession for the Millennium." *Information Highways*, December 1995, 17.

CRISTAL-ED Mailing List. School of Library and Information Studies, University of Michigan. Majordomo@sils.umich.edu http://http2.sils.umich.edu/Publications/CRISTALED/listserv.html

Culnan, Mary J. "What Corporate Librarians Will Need to Know in the Future." *Special Libraries* 77(4), Fall 1986, 213-16.

Dickerson, Mary E., Chair, et al. Presidential Study Commission on Professional Recruitment, Ethics and Professional Standards. The PREPS Commission Report. Washington, DC: SLA, 1992.

Drabenstott, Katherine M. "Analytical Review of the Library of the Future." *College and Research Libraries,* 56(1), January 1995, 89-90.

Drake, Miriam A. "A Special Library Perspective." *Association of Research Libraries: Proceedings of the 124th Annual Meeting,* 1994, p.33-36.

Fisher, William and Matarazzo James. "Professional Development for Special Librarians: Formal Education and Continuous Education for Excellence." In Hill, Linda L., Issue Editor. *Education for Library and Information*

Management Careers in Corporate Environments. *Library Trends,* 42(2), Fall 1993, 290-303.

Griffiths, Jose-Marie and King, Donald W. *Special Libraries: Increasing the Information Edge.* Washington, D.C.: SLA, 1993.

Harris, Gwen and Marshall, Joanne G. "Building a Business Case for Special Library Services: The Case of Current Awareness." *Special Libraries.* 87(3), Summer 1996, 181-94.

Hill, Linda L., Issue Editor. "Education for Library and Information Management Careers in Corporate Environments." *Library Trends,* 42(2), Fall 1993, 225-365.

Horton, Forrest Woody Jr. *Extending the Librarian's Domain: A Survey of Emerging Occupation Opportunities for Librarians and Information Professionals.* Washington, DC: SLA, 1994. (SLA Occasional Paper Series Number Four)

Hunt, Patrick J. "Interpreters as Well as Gatherers: The Librarian of Tomorrow ... Today." *Special Libraries* 86(3), Summer 1995, 195-204.

Johnston, William B. and Arnold H. Packer. *Workforce 2000: Work and Workers for the 21st Century.* Indianapolis: Hudson Institute, 1987.

Keating, Michael. "Corporate Virtual Library: Model for the 1990s." *Business and Finance Division Bulletin,* SLA, 97, Fall 1994, 27.

Kellogg Coalition on Reinventing Information Science, Technology and Library Education (CRISTAL-ED) Project. School of Library and information Studies, University of Michigan. ttp://http2.sils.umich.edu/Publications/CRISTALED/KelloggHomePage.html

Keyes, Alison M. "The Value of the Special Library: Review and Analysis." *Special Libraries* 86(3), Summer 1995, 172-87.

Koenig, Michael E.D. "Educational Requirements for a Library Oriented Career in Information Management." *Library Trends* 42(2), Fall 1993, 277-89.

Malinconico, S. Michael. "What Librarians Need to Know to Survive in an Age of Technology." *Journal of Education for Library and Information Science* 33, Summer, 1992. 226-40.

Martin, Susan K. "Achieving the Vision: Rethinking Librarianship." *Journal of Library Administration* 19(3/4): 209-27, 1993.

Marshall, Joanne G. *The Impact of the Special Library on Corporate Decision-Making.* Washington, DC: SLA, 1993.

Massey-Burzio, Virginia "Education and Experience: Or, the MLS is Not Enough." *RSR: Reference Services Review*. 19(1), 1991, 72-72.

Medical Library Association. *Platform for Change: The Educational Policy Statement of the Medical Library Association*. Chicago: MLA, 1992.

Medical Library Association. *Using Scientific Evidence to Improve Information Practice: The Research Policy Statement of the Medical Library Association*. Chicago: MLA, 1995.

Moulton, Lynda W. "Results of Survey on Professional Development/Graduate Education for Information Professionals." *Library Management Division Quarterly*, SLA, 17(4), Fall 1994, 11-13.

Moulton, Lynda W. "Under Assault? ... Offense, the Best Strategy." *Library Management Division Quarterly*, SLA, 18(1), Spring 1995, 14.

Mount, Ellis, ed. *Opening New Doors: Alternative Careers for Librarians*. Washington, DC: SLA, 1993.

Murphy, Marcy. *The Managerial Competencies of Twelve Corporate Librarians*. Washington, DC: SLA, 1988. (SLA Research Series, Number Two)

Murphy, Marcy. "Preface." In Special Libraries Association. *Future Competencies of the Information Professional*. Washington, DC: SLA, 1991. (SLA Occasional Paper Series, Number One), v-vi.

National Library of Medicine (U.S.). *Planning Panel on the Education and Training of Health Sciences Librarians. The Education and Training of Health Sciences Librarians*. Bethesda, MD: National Institutes of Health, National Library of Medicine, 1995.

Ojala, Marydee. "Core Competencies of Special Librarians of the Future." *Special Libraries*, 84(4), Fall 1993, 230-34.

Ojala, Marydee. "What Will They Call Us in the Future?" *Special Libraries* 84(4), Fall 1994, 226-29.

Paris, Marion and White, Herbert S. "Mixed Signals and Painful Choices: The Education of Special Librarians." *Special Libraries* 77(4), Fall 1986, 207-12.

Piggott, Sylvia E.A. "Why Corporate Librarians Must Reengineer the Library for the New Information Age." *Special Libraries* 86(1), Winter 1995, 11.

Powell, Ronald R and Raber, Douglas. "Education for Reference/Information Service: A Qualitiatative and Quantitative Analysis of Basic Reference Courses." *The Reference Librarian* 43, 1994, 145-72.

Ray, Ron. "Crucial Critics of the Information Age." *Library Journal* 118(7): April 1, 1993, 46-49.

Remeikis, Lois A. "Knowledge Management—Roles for Information Professionals." *Business and Finance Division Bulletin*, SLA, 101, Winter 1996,41-43.

Seiss, Judith. "If I Ruled the World, Library Schools Would..." *Searcher* 2(7), September 1994, 14-16.

Special Libraries Association. *Future Competencies of the Information Professional*. Washington, DC: SLA, 1991. (SLA Occasional Paper Series, Number One)

Special Libraries Association. *Graduate Education Position Statement*. Washington, DC: Professional Development Committee, SLA: 1992. (Reviewed every two years and updated if necessary)

Special Libraries Association. *SLA Research Agenda*. Washington, DC: SLA, 1989.

Special Libraries Association. "Objectives for Special Libraries." *Special Libraries*, 55(10), December 1964, 671-80. (Reprinted as a brochure by SLA)

Special Libraries Association. *Vision Statement*. Washington, DC: SLA, 1989.

Special Libraries Association. *A Visionary Framework for the Future: SLA's Strategic Plan, 1990-2005*. Washington, DC: SLA, 1989.

Spiegelman, Barbara M. "If Practitioners Ruled the World: Suggested Topics for SLA Research." Presented at the conference, *The Future of Research for the Special Library Community*, March, 1995, Chicago, IL.

Tilson, Y. "Income Generation and Pricing in Libraries." *Library Management* 51 (2), 1994, 517.

White, M.D. and Abels, E.G. "Measuring Service Quality in Special Libraries: Lessons from Service Marketing." *Special Libraries* 86(1), Winter 1995, 36-45.

Williamson, Joan. "One-person Libraries and Information Units: Their Education and Training Needs." *Library Management* 9(5), 1-72, 1988.

Zink, Steven D. "Will Librarians Have a Place in the Information Society?" *RSR: Reference Services Review* 19(1), 1991, 76-77.

About the Authors

Mary E. Beall received her master of science degree in Library Science from Wayne State University in Detroit, Michigan. She has worked in the special libraries of an automobile manufacturer, an international labor union, and a litigation consulting firm. In addition, she has worked in information brokerages, served as a visiting lecturer and librarian in government documents for a research university, and was marketing and customer relations assistant for a library reference book publisher. She has served as Government Relations liaison for the Illinois Chapter of the Special Libraries Association for the past two years.

Janice F. Chindlund, native of Ohio, has been involved in business research since 1979. She has served as Head Librarian for an investment advisory business and a global Fortune 500 company, both in greater Chicago. Before earning a master of library and information science degree from Rosary College in 1989, she worked as a business analyst for ten years. Ms. Chindlund earned a B.A. in education from Wheaton College (Illinois). She has been Secretary of the Business & Finance Division of the Special Libraries Association and Co-editor of the Illinois SLA Chapter's bulletin, *Informant*. She currently serves on the Editorial Review Board of *Journal of Business & Finance Librarianship*.

Rebecca S. Corliss has a bachelor's degree in French from the University of Michigan, and studied in France for a year. After obtaining a paralegal degree from the Institute for Paralegal Training in Philadelphia, she worked as paralegal for two years. She was employed as a library assistant in law firms for five years while obtaining a master of library and information science degree from Rosary

College. Since then she has spent six years as a reference librarian in a law firm, and is now Director of Library Services for another firm. Other experience includes a two year stint as a sales representative for a commercial photographer.

Christina M. Krawczyk received her master of arts in library science from Texas Woman's University in 1991, with a minor in business administration, and a B.A. in theatre from Knox College in 1989. She started volunteering in school and public libraries in fourth grade, and has been a professional librarian for six and a half years, with experience in food science, safety/industrial hygiene, and insurance/legal companies. She was President of the Student SLA Chapter at TWU from 1990-1991, and was Chair of the North Suburban Special Librarians Executive Committee from 1995-1996.

Cathy A. Porter has worked in libraries since 1981, beginning her career as an account manager for a library temporary services company. She was a paraprofessional in a financial services company library for three years, has been Head Librarian at that institution since obtaining her master of arts in library science from the University of Chicago in 1990, and is currently working as a solo librarian. Ms. Porter previously studied art and architectural history and has a B.A. in liberal arts from Carleton College in Minnesota.

Sara R. Tompson has worked as an information professional and manager in science libraries (engineering, environmental, and physics) since obtaining a master of science in library and information science degree from the University of Illinois at Urbana-Champaign in 1987. Prior to that, she worked as a paraprofessional in academic libraries. She has contributed articles to such journals as *Science and Technology Libraries* and the *Journal of the American Society for Information Science*. Ms. Tompson has held several professional organization positions, including, Secretary, Illinois Chapter of the Special Libraries Association, Special Libraries Representative to the Lincoln Trail Libraries System Board, and Faculty Advisor to the University of Illinois SLA chapter. Her homepage on the World Wide Web is located at http://www.prairienet.org/ ~stompson/homepage.html.

Lorri A. Zipperer has been in the information business for fifteen years, six as a professional. She received a master of arts in library and information studies from Northern Illinois University in DeKalb in 1991. She has worked in legal, medical, and art museum environments. Her professional activities range from public relations to program development, listserv management to lecturer. Ms. Zipperer was the winner of the 1994 H. W. Wilson Award for article of the year (in *Special Libraries*), has published numerous book reviews and newsletter items, and has edited several reference books in the field of medicine. She has also authored a column reviewing non-clinical web sites for physicians.

Index